Great BRAND Stories

AMERICA

Praise for *America* from the UK *Observer*

Anholt and Hildreth advocate branding as an inherently peaceful and humanistic approach to international relations, because it is based on competition, consumer choice and consumer power. As such it is closely linked to principles of individual freedom and power, far more likely to lead to world peace than statecraft based on territory, economic power, ideologies, politics or religion. They show, too, that brand analysis, because it embraces both emotional and intellectual arguments, has a particular power to put America under a searching spotlight.

America will not only convince you of the serious intent behind [country branding] but will also make you realize that America is indeed the mother of all brands.

John Simmons

Great BRAND Stories

AMERICA

The Mother of All Brands

Simon Anholt
and Jeremy Hildreth

Viva Books
New Delhi | Mumbai | Chennai | Kolkata | Bangalore | Hyderabad | Kochi

First Indian Edition 2009

VIVA BOOKS PRIVATE LIMITED

- 4737/23 Ansari Road, Daryaganj, New Delhi 110 002
  E-mail: vivadelhi@vivagroupindia.net, Tel. 42242200
- 76, Service Industries, Shirvane, Sector 1, Nerul, Navi Mumbai 400 706
  E-mail: vivamumbai@vivagroupindia.net, Tel. 27721273, 27721274
- Jamals Fazal Chambers, 26 Greams Road, Chennai 600 006
  E-mail: vivachennai@vivagroupindia.net, Tel. 28290304, 28294241
- B-103, Jindal Towers, 21/1A/3 Darga Road, Kolkata 700 017
  E-mail: vivakolkata@vivagroupindia.net, Tel. 22836381, 22816713
- 7, Sovereign Park Apartments, 56-58, K. R. Road, Basavanagudi, Bangalore 560 004
  E-mail: vivabangalore@vivagroupindia.net, Tel. 26607409, 26607410
- 101-102 Mughal Marc Apartments, 3-4-637 to 641, Narayanguda, Hyderabad 500 029
  E-mail: vivahyderabad@vivagroupindia.net, Tel. 27564481, 27564482
- Beevi Towers, First Floor, SRM Road, Kaloor, Kochi 682 018, Kerala
  E-mail: vivakochi@vivagroupindia.net, Tel: 0484-2403055, 2403056

www.vivagroupindia.com

Published by arrangement with

Cyan Communications
119, Wardour Street,
London W1F 0UW
UK

ISBN-10: 81-309-0776-3
ISBN-13: 978-81-309-0776-5

Published by Vinod Vasishtha for Viva Books Private Limited, 4737/23, Ansari Road, , Daryaganj, New Delhi-110 002. Printed and bound by Sanat Printers, Kundli - 131 028.

CONTENTS

INTRODUCTION

> **"How is it that the country that invented Hollywood and Madison Avenue has allowed such a destructive and parodied image of itself to become the intellectual coin of the realm overseas?"**
>
> Congressman Henry Hyde

America is not just a country, it is also a brand.

That's not a metaphor, by the way. And it's not one of those games that get played a bit too often in books like this, where you make a parallel between two completely unrelated subjects and hope people will think you're clever. You know – books with titles like *Run your Business like an Ant Colony, All I Really Need to Know I Learned by Watching Cricket, Leadership Secrets of Pine Trees,* etc.

The ways that people all over the world (including in America) think about, talk about and relate to America are exactly the same ways that people think about, talk about and relate to great brands. This is actually true of all countries, but it's especially true of America, because America has quite deliberately and quite consciously built and managed itself as a brand right from the very start.

This book is the first to tell that story. It starts in colonial times and ends with America's current efforts to restore its fading brand image. It draws conclusions about what's gone right, and, more important, wrong.

America today finds itself in an unfamiliar situation. Derided, mistrusted, misunderstood, even hated, it just can't seem to do anything right any more. This sometimes happens to very powerful brands, even when their behaviour is impeccable, which America's hasn't always been.

For reasons both within and beyond its control, America is no longer the ultimate aspirational brand. Tragic is not too strong a word to describe this turn of events.

Because the discipline of branding can take account of both the emotional and the intellectual side of the idea of America, it is uniquely able to explain both the content and the character of America's image, and to chart the rise and decline of Brand America. In fact, without understanding America as a brand, it is very difficult for us to understand the peculiar predicament the country is beset and bewildered by today.

Not everyone is comfortable with the idea that the world's only superpower has much in common with a pair of trainers or a fizzy drink. But bear with us. We're pretty sure that by the end, you'll see America in a rather different light.

1

Let Freedom and Cash Registers Ring: America as a Brand

What is a brand, anyway?

Lots of things are called brands these days. Department stores are brands, companies and universities are brands, singers and sports stars and politicians are brands. Even political parties, religions, cities and nations sometimes get described as brands.

Most people use the term quite loosely, but what they usually mean is that these places, people and organizations have found that their reputation is important to them. They suffer when it's negative and they profit when it's positive, and so they make some attempt to control it. Just like products in a supermarket, the ones with the famous and trusted names are the ones that people choose first, often going to quite a bit of trouble and expense to get hold of them.

And that loose definition of a brand is pretty accurate: at heart, a brand is nothing more and nothing less than the *good name* of something that's on offer to the public.

Obviously, a good name is a valuable thing to have: it's the thing that gets your product noticed and stops it vanishing amid the thousands of nearly identical competing products. It means that when you launch a new product under the same name, people give it a try. It means that people stay loyal to your products, even if, from time to time, they aren't the best, the newest or the easiest to use.

The maker's good name reassures us that time, money and expertise have been invested in making the product as good as possible; it's also a promise that if something goes wrong in a year's time, they'll still be around to put it right.

The brand name acts as our short cut to an informed buying decision. The more often we are proved right about our choice, and the more often the product or service lives up to the good name of the company that makes it, the more valuable that name becomes in our eyes.

Countries as brands

The same principles apply to places. Whether we're thinking about going somewhere on holiday, buying a product that's made in a certain country, applying for a job overseas, moving to a new town, donating money to a war-torn or famine-struck region, or choosing between films or plays or CDs made by artists in different countries, we rely on our perception of those places to make the decision-making process a bit easier, a bit faster, a bit more efficient.

And as with commercial brands, some of the glamour of that place-brand reflects back on us for choosing it. You feel stylish when you become the owner of something by Alessi or Gucci, and you get a similar feeling when you go to the Amalfi coast for your holiday, cook penne all'arrabbiata, take Italian lessons, listen to Pavarotti or name your children Lucia and Stefano.

Some countries – like Italy – add appeal to their exports in a way that seems completely effortless. Even very good products from other places, such as Guatemala or Belgium or Lithuania, somehow don't work the same magic.

Marketing academics call this *country of origin effect.* People have known for centuries that a "Made in..." label is just as powerful and just as valuable as a "Made by..." label. German engineering, French chic, Japanese miniaturization, Italian flair, Swedish design, British class, Swiss precision – these are brand values that rub off onto all the products that come from those countries, and they count for a lot. Country of origin effect is part of the reason why, in the early 1990s, Americans bought lots of Toyota Corollas (which were quite expensive) and not very many Geo Prizms (which were quite cheap), even though they were exactly the same car, made in the same factory. American consumers believed that Japanese cars offered better value than American cars, so they bought the Toyota.

In fact, that reassurance of value or quality that we get from a "Made in" label is really only symbolic. Governments can't impose the same quality standards throughout their entire manufacturing sector, even in very rich (or totalitarian) countries. But faith is often more potent than logic, perception stronger than reality, and this slightly disconcerting observation about human nature is one we will return to more than once during this book.

Country of origin effect is just one aspect of a much bigger and more complex branding phenomenon, and countries behave like brands in lots of other ways. A country's good name doesn't just help consumers make millions of everyday purchasing decisions, it affects much bigger decisions, too: companies deciding where to build their factories, set up their overseas operations, market their products or outsource their industrial processes and customer service centres; governments deciding where to spend their foreign aid budgets; international sporting bodies or beauty contests deciding which country or city will host their next event; opera and theatre companies deciding where to tour; film studios deciding where to go on location; supranational bodies like the European Union, Mercosul, NATO or ASEAN deciding which countries can join and which can't; even governments picking their allies in times of international conflict. It's no exaggeration to say that the brand image of a country has a profound impact on its social, cultural, economic and political destiny.

This is because the organizations that make these big decisions are staffed by people who are still people. They are still consumers in their spare time, they still think like consumers, and even if they're usually anxious to deny it, their choices are affected by their perceptions as well as their expert knowledge. Even though these professional decision makers obviously do go through exhaustive comparisons and analyses of candidate countries, they still need ways to choose between close contenders. In some cases, a bribe will do the trick, but the brand images of countries are equally good at "unsticking" these difficult decisions.

The decision makers know that their decision has to be the right one for an end user too. Using facts alone to pick the host country for an international sporting event is fine up to a point, but in the end, it has to be a location that the television audience finds exciting and appealing. Athletes and spectators have to feel happy about travelling and staying there, and their perceptions or prejudices about the place will carry just as much weight as practical considerations such as cost, transport links and facilities.

The same applies when multinational companies are deciding where to build their overseas offices or factories. Their management may well choose a country on the basis of its infrastructure, climate, location, security, transport links, supplier firms' quality and location, business-friendly government, tax breaks and incentive packages, but it's still the wrong decision if the staff who actually have to relocate there don't fancy the sound of that particular country. And even if they can be persuaded, can their families?

It's surprising to discover how big a part is played by "mere" image or reputation in these decisions. A paper by researchers John Pantzalis and Carl A. Rodrigues showed that investors are often heavily influenced by countries' brands, which in turn affects the movement of international capital in and out of those countries. [1] Investors might, for instance, group several countries together because of superficial brand associations. The Asian Tigers sounded like a good bet, but in fact some of the countries thus branded shouldn't really have been in the group at all, and made a lot of people lose a lot of money.

Another example of the power of faith over logic, and how reputation can carry more weight than practical considerations, was the diplomatic success of Benjamin Franklin, a man who features prominently in the next chapter. He communicated his

[1] Endnotes appear on pp. 181–3.

personal brand to the French so effectively that his word alone was enough to set them at war with the British:

> Men imagined they saw in him a sage of antiquity, come back to give austere lessons and generous examples to the moderns. They personified in him the republic of which he was the representative and the legislator. They regarded his virtues as those of his countrymen, and even judged of their physiognomy by the imposing and serene traits of his own... After this picture, it would be useless to trace the history of Franklin's negotiations with the court of France. His virtues and his renown negotiated for him; and before the second year of his mission had expired, no one conceived it possible to refuse fleets and an army to the compatriots of Franklin. [2]

Of course, there's nothing scandalous or mysterious about any of this. We are creatures who can experience the world only through our perceptions of it. The distinction between perception and reality is not a sharply drawn line at all when you start to think about it, but a rather hazy philosophical distinction.

So how are those country images created?

It's almost always a mixture of the deliberate and the accidental, the fair and the unfair. Most countries send out messages about themselves most of the time, via a "hexagon" of communication channels and actions and behaviours, and it's the cumulative effect of these which, over the years, creates their brands. We'll use this model throughout the book.

Countries can influence their brand image if they have a good, clear, believable idea of what they really stand for, and if this message comes out clearly and consistently through some or all

THE POINTS OF THE HEXAGON

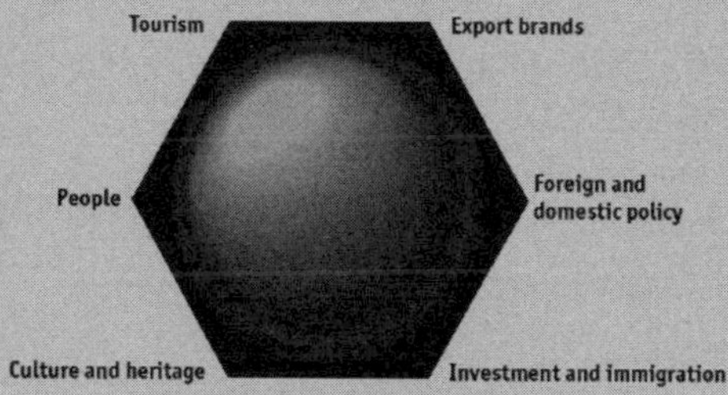

- The country's tourism promotion, and people's experience of visiting the country as tourists or business travellers. This is often the loudest voice in branding the nation because the tourist board usually has the biggest budgets and the best marketers.
- The country's exports, which are powerful ambassadors of the country's image abroad, but only when it's clearly stated where they are made.
- The policy decisions of the country's government. Policy is traditionally communicated through diplomatic channels, but policy makers are much closer to the international media than they used to be.
- To business audiences, the way the country attracts inward investment, foreign talent and foreign companies.
- The country's cultural activities and exports: a world tour by a national opera company, the works of a famous author, the national sports team.
- The people of the country themselves: the high-profile leaders, media and sports stars and the general population; how they behave when abroad and how they treat visitors at home.

Source: www.placebrands.net / © 2003 Placebrands Ltd

points of the hexagon. And there are good reasons for countries to try to do this, because a powerful and positive national brand benefits exporters, importers, government, the culture sector, tourism, immigration and pretty much every aspect of international relations.

Governments understand this very well, and most of them are now trying or have tried in the past to achieve some kind of control over their images. A few countries have succeeded: Ireland, Spain, New Zealand, South Africa and Scotland have improved their images in a fairly short time, to the great benefit of their economic health and self-respect. Lots of others continue to work on the problem: Australia, India, Russia, Wales, Taiwan, Croatia, Slovenia, Estonia, South Korea, Britain and a number of much poorer countries too.

Then there's a handful of megabrand countries – Japan, Germany, Italy, Switzerland and France – with images so powerful and so positive, you might think they hardly need to bother managing them (in fact, few of them do, at least not in an energetic or systematic way). These countries are effortlessly synonymous with a number of valuable attributes (France for chic and quality of living, Italy for style and sexiness, Germany for quality engineering, Switzerland for purity, wealth and integrity, Japan for technology, entertainment, design and style), and each time a new brand emerges from one of them, it seems to have a head start over all its competitors in the global marketplace.

The big one

And way ahead of the megabrands, Brand America is in a class of its own.

If we begin with its power as a country of origin, "Made in America" is a premium label in an incredibly wide range of product and service sectors.

Products from America simply need to state their country of origin (though not all of the brands in the box do), and a cultural and commercial trail is blazed for them around the world. Little wonder that so many brands from other countries are keen to borrow American attributes: there are hundreds of pseudo-American brands around the world that have prospered for years by pirating a little of the equity of Brand America. Brooklyn chewing gum, for instance, has been the market leader for fifty years in Italy, despite the fact that it is made by the Perfetti company of Milan and has nothing whatever to do with America.

International brand consultancy Interbrand and *Business Week* publish an annual report on the world's top 100 brands, and America dominates the table every year, producing ten times more billion-dollar brands than any other country. Out of the 100 most valuable global brands, 64 are American owned.

But commercial brands are only one point of the hexagon of place branding. America comfortably dominates the whole spectrum of national image, from its massive trade presence in both imports and exports to foreign policy, where, like it or not, it has the loudest voice and the clearest brand. In international cultural activity and cultural influence, no other country comes close to America's dominance – some would say its stranglehold – over global television, cinema, music, book and magazine publishing and internet presence. American people, famous and not, are everywhere, and act as powerful communicators of Brand

WHERE BRAND AMERICA LEADS

1. **The definitive youth lifestyle:** Coke, Pepsi, MTV, Wrigley's, Levi's, Wrangler, OshKosh, Fender, Gibson.
2. **The definitive older male lifestyle:** Marlboro, Camel, Zippo, Budweiser, Michelob, Coors, Jim Beam, Southern Comfort, Jack Daniel's, Winston, Dockers, Lucky Strike, Harley-Davidson, Ray-Ban, Winchester, Colt.
3. **Sporting prowess:** Nike, O'Neill, Reebok, NBA, Champion USA, Weider.
4. **Technological supremacy:** IBM, Compaq, Oracle, Dell, Cisco, Palm, Hewlett-Packard, AT&T, Apple, Motorola, Intel, DuPont, Lycra, Microsoft, Texas Instruments, Dolby, Xerox, Bose, Whirlpool, Maytag, 3M.
5. **Engineering supremacy:** Caterpillar, John Deere, DeWalt, McCulloch, Black & Decker, Boeing, Ford, Chevrolet, General Motors, Chrysler, Lockheed, Firestone.
6. **Energy:** Chevron-Texaco, Mobil, Exxon, General Electric, Duracell, Edison.
7. **The great outdoors:** Timberland, Rockport, Columbia, Coleman, Jeep.
8. **Fun and leisure:** Disney, Kodak, Nickelodeon, Sesame Street, Warner Bros, Pixar, DreamWorks, Mattel, The Simpsons, Hasbro, Universal Studios, Planet Hollywood, A&M, Atlantic Records, Decca, Motown, RCA, eBay, AOL, Yahoo!, Electronic Arts, Marvel, Xbox, Fox, MGM.

9. **Retail:** Wal-Mart, Woolworth, Amazon, Tower Records, Safeway, Tandy.
10. **Travel:** Hilton, Hertz, Marriott, Avis, Budget, Alamo, Holiday Inn, Sheraton, FedEx.
11. **Information:** CNN, Time, Newsweek, Discovery, National Geographic, NBC, Bloomberg, Webster.
12. **Domestic and personal hygiene:** Pledge, Fairy, Listerine, Colgate-Palmolive, Crest, Jacuzzi, Pampers, Kleenex, Gillette, Oral-B, Sensodyne, Ultrabrite, Johnson & Johnson, Ajax, Glade, Ariel, Bounce, Dash/Daz.
13. **Health:** Merck, Pfizer, Eli Lilly, Vicks, Sudafed, Zantac, Anacin/Anadin, Halls, Immodium, Benylin, Tylenol, Benadril, Advil, Actifed.
14. **Wealth:** American Express, Chase Manhattan, Merrill Lynch, J. P. Morgan, Goldman Sachs, Forbes, Citibank, Diners Club, Morgan Stanley, Western Union.
15. **Fashion:** Calvin Klein, Donna Karan, Tommy Hilfiger, Ralph Lauren, Gap, Tiffany, Playtex.
16. **Beauty:** Elizabeth Arden, Revlon, Max Factor, Avon, Clinique, Head & Shoulders, Alberto V05, Camay, Estée Lauder, Oil of Olay/Olaz.
17. **Food:** McDonald's, NutraSweet, Campbell's, Tropicana, Del Monte, Ben & Jerry's, Kellogg's, Heinz, Mars, Burger King, Starbucks, Uncle Ben's, Doritos, Pizza Hut, Pillsbury, KFC, Taco Bell, Weight Watchers, Kraft.

America in everything they do and say. Part of the reason they do this so well is because they love their country so much; more on this later.

Brand America is so powerful, in fact, that it shares an unusual characteristic with the world's greatest commercial brand. Just like Coca-Cola (aka Coke), America (aka the United States) manages to be known the world over by *two different brand names,* a trick that most brand consultants would strongly advise against, though it apparently does nothing to weaken the impact of either.

Mind control?

Managing a brand doesn't mean controlling the consumer. Madonna can't make you like her music, or force you to think of her as fashionable, but she can and does work to project a certain image of herself. Volkswagen doesn't and can't dictate what people think of its wagons, but it certainly tries to influence the idea of Volkswagen that people have in their minds.

Not everything that affects a nation's brand is done with the deliberate intention of influencing it. A lot can happen by accident, and deliberate actions often have unintended consequences. Putting a man on the moon may not have been intended as an advertisement for American technology, but it certainly worked as one, and Brand America was credited with the achievement. NASA isn't, strictly speaking, a sales promotion agency for American technology, any more than Hollywood is the advertising agency for American values, culture and tourism, but both have always performed these roles with vigour and effectiveness.

Meanwhile, from the partly intentional to the absolutely deliberate, America has done more to control its reputation than any other place in history. In war and in peace, through words and actions, inside and outside its borders, it has done so from its earliest days. Today, there is no person, place or thing that has managed to achieve a recognition as wide, as deep, as lasting and as powerful as that of the United States of America. To a villager in Papua New Guinea, a taxi driver in Mumbai or a hairdresser in Latvia, America stands for pretty much the same things.

Liberty has been the main idea behind Brand America since the dawn of the nation; America is basically *about* freedom. The idea of freedom was particularly potent during the 1940s, 1950s and 1960s: for millions of people abroad, emerging from the shadow of fascism, communism or the nightmare of two world wars, the idea of a country where cowboys roamed free, went to bed when they wanted, drank coffee at all hours and never washed behind their ears seemed like paradise.

And the idea of a land of opportunity shows a wonderful grasp of consumer psychology. It's a flattering idea that the country you've been living in up until now is really to blame for your lack of success; once you get to America, your natural talents will at last find free expression and you will fulfil your natural potential. Like all wonderful advertising promises, it's effective because there's an element of truth in it: it's an exaggeration, not a lie.

The idea of a place where you can achieve great wealth without great exertion has been a fixation of mankind since the beginning of time, and the role of Eldorado for the modern world was a natural one for America. Thanks to wild tales before Columbus, enthusiastic promotion of the colonies, well-written romances of successful pioneering, news of the gold rush and the appeal of icons like the American entrepreneur creating fabulous wealth from humble beginnings in his garage, the American millionaire making a killing on Wall Street and the American multinational corporation straddling the globe – all faithfully portrayed through Hollywood – most people in most countries still think first of money when they think of America.

In Italy, they still use the word *America* to mean any kind of utopia. *Non é l'America,* people sometimes say modestly about their home town: *it's not America,* meaning *it's hardly paradise,* or *crede di aver trovato l'America: he thinks he's found America,* meaning *he thinks he's found a way to make his fortune.* You can find similar sayings all over the world, wherever there has been a tradition of emigration to that promised land.

Money and freedom. Or, if you look at it another way, free money: the oldest advertising ploy in the book. It's not surprising that America has kept such a tight grip on the world's imagination for so long.

Even the bad bits sometimes seem to help the good bits: the negative elements in America's reputation, such as drugs, crime and violence (again, sometimes deliberately and sometimes casually portrayed by Hollywood and the American global news media), are exactly the sort to stimulate prickly teenagers and young adults, who naturally aspire to have the opposite values from their parents, and preferably to alarm them as much as possible.

But some new negative ideas have recently started to join the list of things that America stands for, and it's hard to see how they could add anything to the country's overall image: America as bullying, polluting, domineering, imperialistic, ignorant, fat, selfish, inconsistent, arrogant, self-absorbed, greedy, hypocritical and meddling. We'll come back to this later.

The natural

America has taken so naturally to being a nation brand partly because it has always been a country that *stands* for things, both for itself and for other people. It has always been fond of big ideas. It's a country that has always liked to feel that its actions reflect deeply held beliefs about itself and about the way the world works, or should work. Ever since it submitted its case for independence to the tribunal of the world, America has tried to justify its actions, especially its foreign policy, in terms of philosophical rationales, grand doctrines and sweeping ideals. So keeping peace and cooperation among nations, holding communism at bay and relieving the Middle East of a mad regime become "Wilsonian idealism," the "doctrine of containment" and "Operation Enduring Freedom."

Powerful brands need symbols, and America is no exception. You could write a book (perhaps somebody already has) about how America has been officially represented in images, from its eagles and Great Seal to its monuments and buildings, and especially its flag. The Stars and Stripes is far more important to Americans than flags are to people in most other countries. Every time a US senator is interviewed on TV, there's a flag behind him – something that Americans hardly notice because it's so familiar, but foreign audiences are always struck by it. And one of the first things tourists notice when travelling around America is how many houses, shop windows, petrol station forecourts, local police uniforms, jogging shorts and 18-wheeler mud flaps are adorned with Old Glory or some variant of it.

In America, buildings, places, quotations, animals, products, foods, days in the year, poems, movies, novels and songs are all national symbols. One of the reasons, apparently, why many Americans were offended by the sexual misconduct of President Clinton was because it happened not in a hotel, or even in a bedroom in the White House, but right in the Oval Office. In the minds of many, this was desecrating a symbol of the presidency, with all the authority and high-minded values that it represents. And when comedienne Roseanne Arnold performed a deliberately awful rendition of the national anthem at a baseball game some years ago, she had hell to pay for it. In fact, the very act of singing the national anthem before a game – which is by no means the custom in every country – is another example of the strong national feeling that underpins and continually reinforces America's idea of itself.

This (usually) benign nationalism is the country branding equivalent of what Nicholas Ind called "living the brand" in his book of the same name. If the staff don't share the values of the corporation, then they are unlikely to do their jobs properly or treat customers in the right way. And unless there's some sense of shared values and common purpose, the corporation will never develop that coherent identity that the customer will recognize as a brand.

Another reason why America has become such a strong brand is because marketing, advertising, branding, sales promotion, TV and radio spots, direct mail, catalogue selling, point of sale, the internet, consumer research, focus groups, public relations and the whole shooting-match of commercial publicity were invented in America. Commerce is an inextricable part of the American identity, and the weapons of commerce have always been a part of the armoury of the American empire. Doing business is as American as apple pie. Buying and selling come as second nature to Americans, and salesmanship and entrepreneurialism are qualities that all Americans understand, accept and admire.

It's a far cry from many countries in Western Europe, where selling is considered to be slightly vulgar and marketing a kind of devilry. The worst insult that Napoleon could allegedly think of levelling at the British was that they were a nation of shopkeepers, and the French advertising legend Jacques Séguéla entitled his 1979 autobiography *Don't Tell My Mother I Work in Advertising: She Thinks I Play Piano in a Brothel.* In this respect, America has more in common with the Middle East and Asia, where commerce has always been thought of as a dignified, even a princely activity.

For these and many other reasons, America has attended to its image and reputation right from the beginning. From the colonial days through to the Civil War, from cultural exchanges to covert operations during the Cold War, from the Voice of America to CNN, from World War I propaganda to the recent attempts of advertising heroine Charlotte Beers to influence Arab and world opinion over terrorism and Iraq, the efforts of America to orchestrate its national reputation have never let up. Throughout its history, America has been conscious – sometimes hyper-conscious – of its reputation, and has frequently had people on the payroll whose job descriptions sound remarkably like that of a Procter & Gamble brand manager.

It's a long and complex tale featuring some odd events and still odder characters, but the story of how Brand America has been built is truly heroic. And it must be said that this is a brand that has been managed for the most part with honour and integrity, or at least with the best intentions, as well as skill, inventiveness, vigour, consistency and passion, for a quarter of a millennium.

All the more pity, then, that the past few years have seen such a decline in the passion, consistency, vigour, inventiveness, skill, integrity *and* honour with which it has been managed. But that's a matter for the last chapter. For now, we need to travel back to the eighteenth century, and witness the birth of Brand America.

2

Brand of the Free:

Launching Brand America

"The life of nations no less than that of men is lived largely in the imagination."

Enoch Powell

Not interested

One of the first things you learn in marketing is that the people you're talking to are usually far less interested in you than you are. Like a lot of marketing advice, this applies to most situations where you need to communicate with a large number of people.

And that's the reason why marketing messages need to be simple, whether it's a slogan to sell a tin of beans, or a statement of national identity designed to sway the world to your values. A second of somebody's attention is a precious thing in a busy world. We are all good at ignoring because we live in a world where we are bombarded by messages, and unless we screen out the stuff that is worthless or irrelevant, we drown in information.

The way brands work in these hostile conditions will sound familiar to most of us. It's like when you spot somebody attractive in a dark, noisy bar, and if you're lucky you have one sentence to persuade them that it's worth going outside for a proper chat. (And the bar is crowded with people who are just as fascinating as you.)

That little sentence, and the way it's delivered, are therefore critical. If it works, then the person or product or country has a chance to get a dialogue going, and if the "customer" likes what he or she finds on closer acquaintance, real understanding and familiarity may follow.

Liberty is a simple idea to build a country on and attract people to, but it's also an idea that by the eighteenth century had been bandied about a lot. So even in its early days, America always needed new, arresting and unforgettable ways of presenting it.

In November 1751, the Pennsylvania Assembly placed an order with London's Whitechapel Foundry for a 2,000 pound bell. They wanted it for their new statehouse in Philadelphia, which was then under construction. The statehouse would become known as Independence Hall because it was here,

25 years later, that delegates to the Continental Congress from the 13 colonies gathered to foment revolution. And the bell would for ever be known as the Liberty Bell, after the words engraved upon it:

> PROCLAIM LIBERTY THROUGHOUT ALL THE LAND UNTO ALL THE INHABITANTS THEREOF.

Let freedom ring

Liberty, with all its political, social, economic and moral implications, came to be recognized as the central idea of America. But it was clear from the start that liberty would never be universally adopted or accepted unless the people of the emerging nation were united enough to believe in it.

At this time, of course, America wasn't a cohesive unit but a collection of independent colonies that Britain, France and Spain fought over as they competed for territorial control. Before America could become the America we know, these scores had to be settled.

Union was necessary for building what we would today call a single brand vision, and union was what Benjamin Franklin had in mind when he produced the famous "Join, or Die" device in 1754 as part of his campaign to unite the colonies with Britain in common defence against the French.

This simple woodcut is, by any definition, an advertisement: not the first case of political advertising in history, but a fine example of the art. To take a complex argument and turn it into a simple two-way choice without trivializing it; to illustrate it with an unusual and memorable visual device; and to finish it off with a punchy, equally memorable slogan – that's exactly the

CORBIS

combination that advertising creatives still aspire to achieve today. Not for the last time, America found the leadership it wanted in a man who was a brilliant salesman of ideas. "We must hang together," intoned Franklin later on, "or assuredly we will all hang separately."

But advertising was already a familiar concept to Americans, even if some of the goods on sale were of dubious value compared to union or liberty. An advertisement from a Philadelphia newspaper on 19 August 1731 reads: "The Widow READ, removed from the upper End of Highstreet to the *New Printing-Office* near the Market, continues to make and sell her well-known Ointment for the ITCH... It is always effectual for that purpose, and never fails to perform the Cure speedily. It also kills or drives away all Sorts of Lice... It has no offensive Smell, but rather a pleasant one; and may be used without the least Apprehension of Danger, even to a sucking Infant... Price 2 s. a Gallypot containing an Ounce." [3]

Advertising was also a familiar concept to Franklin, literally: the newspaper was the *Pennsylvania Gazette,* its publisher was

Bettmann/CORBIS

And they meant it.

Benjamin Franklin, and the Widow Read was Franklin's mother-in-law. [4]

As the prospect of a reconciliation with Britain receded, the colonists began to identify less strongly with Britain. More and more non-British symbols began to appear in the colonies (such as the predecessors of the first Navy Jack flag, which was adorned with 13 stripes, a rattlesnake and the slogan "Don't tread on me") as the American self-concept grew stronger. Richard L. Merritt has attempted to measure how the idea of American-ness spread in the colonies by examining the use of symbols during the period: between 1735 and the early 1760s, only about 6.5 percent of the flags and other symbols used in America identified the population as American. [5] After the imposition of the Sugar Act, the Stamp Act, the Townshend Act, the Tea Act and a series of so-called Intolerable Acts (a bit of pro-revolutionary branding in that name), the use of explicitly American symbols rose rapidly in the mid-1760s to between 50 and 60 percent, and stayed at that level throughout the Revolution.

In a similar way, modern corporations need to rationalize and harmonize their visual identity if they are to get a grip on their brands. Exactly 200 years after the Jay treaty declared "a firm, inviolable and universal peace, and a true and sincere friendship between His Britannic Majesty, his heirs and successors, and the United States of America," signalling the completion of the "demerger" of America and Britain, Lou Gerstner took over as chief executive of IBM. One of his first actions on taking up the post was to impose a single corporate identity and logo on the organization.

Before Gerstner's arrival, there were almost as many different logos and business-card designs as there were IBM offices around the world. At first, many saw their new CEO as a man tinkering with the symptoms instead of tackling the disease, but anybody who understands the ways brands work for corporations will know that a common visual identity is a fundamental part of teaching a large organization to think of itself as one, and behave accordingly. Unlike the adoption of American symbols in eighteenth-century flags, this was entirely deliberate, but the principle behind it was the same: people need an image to gather around.

Ironically, says Samuel P. Huntington, author of *The Clash of Civilizations*, the British identified the land and its people as American before the Americans did. The reason for this, according to the historian John M. Murrin, is that "the British worried about the whole because they did not understand the parts, and they reified their concerns into a totality they called America... in a word, America was Britain's idea." [6]

And this is often the way with brands: a brand is the sum of an external observer's associations with the product or organization, so the only place where the brand truly exists is in the consumer's mind. Sometimes you need this distance and objectivity to see the wood for the trees; people in a factory may find it hard to describe the image of their organization, but consumers generally don't have much difficulty.

Whether America was Britain's idea or not, by the summer of 1776, America had its own idea of what it wanted to be. America saw itself as different from Britain, and wanted to *be* different from Britain.

We should all be so lucky

Not many organizations are perceptive or committed enough to work out their big idea and build it into their group culture as soon as they launch, but when they do it gives them a flying start and a sense of purpose that cuts a swathe through the market-place. In the history of nations, only America and a handful of other countries have had the opportunity as well as the wisdom to do the equivalent thing and put their brand strategy, their public and private purpose, in writing right at the start.

The task of writing the Declaration of Independence fell to a 34-year-old redheaded Virginian named Thomas Jefferson. Jefferson sat with a dipping pen and a few sheaves of paper at a small desk that he had designed himself several years earlier, in a house on the southwest corner of 7th and Market Street in Philadelphia, a few blocks from Pennsylvania Statehouse and directly across the street from a reeking stable. For all his complaints about them, the horseflies that were drawn to the stable did not deter or distract him from his task.

The result of Jefferson's labours is one of the most moving and significant short pieces of prose ever written. As a press release to announce the launch of a hitherto unknown venture called the United States of America, nothing any PR agency has done since has bettered it in style or impact. Together with the Constitution drawn up 13 years later, it lays out the brand values of the nation and explains to the world how America should be understood: as an entirely new kind of country whose government depends for its legitimacy on the support of the governed, and which defines itself in frankly ideological terms as pro-liberty and anti-tyranny.

Marketing is a set of techniques that is mainly used to help companies sell things more effectively, and it may seem strange to draw parallels between such a humble pursuit and the birth of a great nation. But the fact is that whenever human beings form themselves into groups, whether it's political parties, armies, nations or corporations, the same forces rule and the same rules apply.

The instinctive understanding of such principles by natural marketers like Jefferson contributed a quality of practical, rigorous, egalitarian, quick-witted humanism to American policy during its formative stages that set the tone for much of what was to follow.

An American in Paris

Abroad, the ideological stand taken in the Declaration met with instant and enthusiastic approval. When Benjamin Franklin arrived in France in December 1776 to seek recognition of the United States as an independent country, he was happy to report back to Congress that "It is a common observation here that our cause is the cause of all mankind, and that we are fighting for their liberty in defending our own." [7]

But it took more than ideological empathy to persuade the French to join the colonists' fight against Britain. Fortunately for America, Franklin – at the time the most famous American in the world because of his electrical exploits – was the best imaginable man for the job. "To the French," writes Walter Isaacson,

Franklin's biographer and a former chairman of CNN, "this lightning-defying scientist and tribune of liberty who had unexpectedly appeared on their shores was a symbol both of the virtuous frontier freedom romanticized by Rousseau and of the Enlightenment's reasoned wisdom championed by Voltaire." [8]

Franklin understood what people sometimes call self-branding: the need to be a bit larger than life in public affairs, and to be known for a few remarkable attributes that add up to a unique, compelling and unforgettable whole. He has been characterized as "America's first great publicist, [who] was, in his life and in his writings, consciously trying to create a new American archetype." One wouldn't wish to question Franklin's scientific and philosophical integrity, but a certain experiment with a kite, a key and a length of wire could almost have been calculated to establish him as a figure of fabulous power and courage: a human conductor of lightning, no less.

In their book *Managing Brand Me: How to Build your Personal Brand,* Thomas Gad and Annette Rosencreutz point out that "the most successful personal brand builders ... all have one thing in common: there are a lot of good stories about them. These stories are filled with symbols and rituals that these people enact to create a place in people's minds." Gad and Rosencreutz also stress the importance of dramatizing the key attributes of your personal brand identity to make them striking and memorable. These techniques have been used, deliberately or unconsciously, by virtually every significant political, social, spiritual and commercial leader in America's history, and the ones that haven't used them haven't usually become significant.

Branding is full of human epithets – brand personality, brand identity, on-brand behaviour, brand character, brand voice – because the way people form relationships with brands is similar to the way they form them with people. So to have a real person fronting a brand can help add depth and richness to people's perception of it. Endowing a product or a country with enough depth and richness for consumers to like and trust it can take a long time; representing it by a real person whose well-known qualities are transferred to the brand can speed up the process considerably.

Identifying a brand with a person brings risks as well as rewards, though. The actors' adage "Never work with children and animals" (presumably because you never quite know what they are going to do next) also applies to brand spokesmen, especially if they have the larger-than-life personalities that make them effective icons. O. J. Simpson and Michael Jackson spring to mind, not to mention a couple of recent US presidents.

If they fulfil this demanding role well, such men and women become a tough act to follow. When Thomas Jefferson took over as ambassador from Franklin in 1785, he was greeted by the French foreign minister Vergennes with the question: "It is you who replace Dr Franklin?" To which Jefferson replied: "No one can replace him, sir; I am only his successor."

But if the underlying brand values and the corporate culture of the workforce are strong enough, the brand will continue to prosper and carry on to its next great figurehead, even if there is a bit of a gap before he or she turns up.

Americans have always found it easiest to feel comfortable with business when there's a real person out front: from Cornelius Vanderbilt, J. Pierpont Morgan, Henry Ford, John D. Rockefeller and Andrew Carnegie through to Lee Iacocca, Donald Trump, Lou Gerstner, Jack Welch and Larry Ellison. The same has always applied to politics too. This personal brand value is so important that it is quite common, at least in politics, for a political naïf to be elected just because of their salesmanship and their larger-than-life stature. After all, policy knowledge, speech writing and the like can be supported by a team of backroom advisors, a tactic used by Sonny Bono and Arnold

Schwarzenegger, amongst others. It's worth pointing out that this is the exact opposite of the Soviet model of faceless, unbranded state institutions fronted by characterless officials – perhaps one reason why the whole notion of communism was so unappealing to Americans.

Franklin undoubtedly united many qualities in one man, being statesman, diplomat, philosopher and communicator, and he was idolized both at home and abroad in a way that seems impossible to equal today.

The word gets out

America was a new kind of country. To borrow the term of Rosser Reeves, one of the founding fathers of American advertising, America had the unique selling proposition to end all USPs. The simple, compelling brand truth was beginning to pay off, and people flocked to it from all over the world. In the beginning, they were escaping from the troubles of the old world without the faintest idea what they'd find in the new one. Later, when the word got out about the benefits of life in America, people started coming because of what they expected to find, and the numbers continued to increase.

One of those settlers was Normandy-born and ornately named J. Hector St John de Crevecoeur, who embarked for America in 1754, purchased an estate in Pennsylvania, and married the daughter of an American merchant. In his *Letters from an American Farmer*, first published in 1782 in English and translated soon after into French, Crevecoeur described his adoptive country and his countrymen in the most flattering terms:

> We are the most perfect society now existing in the world.... Here individuals of all nations are melted

> into a new race of men, whose labours and posterity will one day cause great changes in the world.... Here a man is free as he ought to be.... An American is a new man, who acts upon new principles; he must therefore entertain new ideas, and form new opinions. From involuntary idleness, servile dependence, penury, and useless labour, he has passed to toils of a very different nature, rewarded by ample subsistence – this is an American.

It was partly through such fervent testimonies from men like Crevecoeur, and from foreigners like the even more famous Frenchman de Tocqueville and the less famous German Francis Lieber, that America gained its reputation abroad, because third-party endorsements *work.* This is also why the words of hundreds of later commentators such as Charles Dickens and P. G. Wodehouse have always carried such weight and have achieved so much to build the image of Brand America.

If, as Huntington writes, "the seventeenth- and eighteenth-century settlers came to America because it was *tabula rasa,*" the later settlers came because they were attracted by the Brand of the Free, and they wanted a piece of it. What Huntington describes as the "American Creed with its principles of liberty, equality, individualism, representative government, and private property" has not usually been seen by historians as a marketing tool, but it certainly worked as one.

To immigrants, the brand promise of America was simple: if you were willing to be industrious and reasonably virtuous, you could rise in wealth and status in America as you could nowhere else on earth. Marketers today often describe brands as representing a lifestyle that people aspire to; America may be the original aspirational brand.

Consider too the way that America has lived up to its reputation as a melting pot. Despite wave upon wave of immigrants breaking over its shores, America's core identity has remained solid. "Subsequent generations of immigrants were assimilated into the culture of the founding settlers and contributed to and modified it," writes Huntington. "But they did not change it fundamentally."

It's not stretching a point to compare this with the culture of successful corporations. When the shared identity and corporate culture are strong enough, the company will keep its essential character through many changes of personnel, management and even chief executive. That sense of common purpose is vital for *esprit de corps* and to maintain that consistent experience for the consumer that is so crucial to business success. In the same way, America is still decidedly America under George W. Bush as it was under Abraham Lincoln, just as Hewlett-Packard is still HP under Carly Fiorina as it was under Bill Hewlett and Dave Packard. The reason and the method are the same: a clear and clearly communicated set of underlying principles that are seldom if ever changed and vigorously and ritually repeated; and powerful mechanisms for ensuring that the basic components of the shared culture and purpose remain constant from one location and generation to the next.

These principles – building and preserving a unified group culture rather than a mix of different cultures; fostering a sense of common purpose where personal ambition is harmonized with shared goals and loyalty to the group; adhering rigorously to internal and external branding – are not things that American bosses or management consultants plucked out of the air one day because they seemed like a good idea. Rather, they learned them from the society in which they were born and raised.

The great American corporations have expanded across the world acquiring foreign companies or competing against them so effectively that the whole business culture in other countries has had to adopt the same principles in order to withstand the onslaught. In this way, the American way of doing business has become the dominant global model. Even something as apparently insignificant as Microsoft's PowerPoint, adopted worldwide as the standard business presentation tool, has had a profound influence, Americanizing not just the structure and style of business strategy presentations around the world, but to some extent the structure and style of the strategies themselves.

American social and ideological values have influenced American corporate practices and values, and those American corporate practices and values in turn have a social and ideological influence on the countries that adopt them. Today, commercial practice influences many other areas of life, so the American-inspired commercial models have a very broad impact. In fact, the idea of nation branding itself, which stems from a very American mixture of marketing, politics and international relations, is a good example of this. It is one of the many ways in which the American brand and its values continue their relentless international expansion.

Expansion and empire

As America grew in territory and population, its sub-brands began to develop. Just as Procter & Gamble have Pringles, Head & Shoulders and Crest, so America had California, Texas, New England, the Prairies, the Rockies, the West and many more. Like all good brands, these were more than just names: they soon became shorthand for the ideas and values and ways of life they represented. Such evocative images as gold prospectors, the Alamo and cowboys and Indians have captured the imaginations of millions, and have become so intrinsic to the idea of America that it is impossible to imagine America without them. This is just as true for Americans as it is for foreigners: the American sense of identity has always been inspired and informed by ideas of a pioneering spirit, Yankee ingenuity and frontier justice.

And these are ideas that remain salient. George W. Bush has been accused of acting like an Old West gunslinger (a role that Ronald Reagan acted more literally). Westerns such as the 1962 movie *The Man Who Shot Liberty Valance* "perfectly reflect," says Monteagle Stearns, American Foreign Service officer and former ambassador to Greece, "what might be termed the iconographic American view of conflict, conflict resolution, and diplomacy." [9]

The sub-brands of Brand America still see themselves as brands today. During the past ten years, just about every state of the union, and almost every major city, has hired advertising or branding or PR agencies to work on their brands and develop new logos, slogans and ad campaigns – and the competition between them for investment, tourists, jobs, talent and attention grows fiercer every year.

Two hundred years ago, the most problematic brand extension for America was the Confederate States of America, formed when eleven southern states seceded from the United States over a number of issues including slavery, which the South supported and the North generally did not.

The Confederacy brand, it turned out, had the wrong stuff both in its core identity (pro-slavery) and how it represented itself to the world (poor diplomacy): it was arguably a bad product with bad marketing. But in some ways it was a successful brand: the Confederate flag still stands for states' rights and hardcore liberty, or simple southern pride. The shell of a once-living brand, in fact, is all that's left of the CSA.

For Brand America, the Civil War was a turning point. Afterwards, regionalism receded, full nationhood took the place of expedient union, and Americans began to see themselves as a single people sharing common values. By the end of the Civil

John Van Hasselt/CORBIS SYGMA

The Confederacy's symbolism has outlasted its reality by almost 150 years.

War, Brand America was ready to begin its global expansion, united under one flag and under one great purpose – or rather one and a half great purposes: liberty, and the pursuit of wealth.

But rather than attempt to conquer the world by force, as other great nations had before it, America was going to make people want to *buy*. In his inaugural address as John Adams successor, Thomas Jefferson had called for "peace, commerce, and honest friendship with all nations, entangling alliances with none" – and you can't help noticing that commerce came second in the list after peace (perhaps because you can't have commerce without it).

Joseph Nye, a political scientist and dean of Harvard University's Kennedy School of Government, draws a distinction between the "soft" and "hard" powers of nations. There are times when only coercion can achieve the aims that a government rightly or wrongly wishes to pursue: this is hard power. Other ends can be attained only through the exercise of cultural, intellectual or spiritual influence: soft power. As Nye says, "a country may obtain the outcomes it wants in world politics because other countries want to follow it, admiring its values, emulating its example, aspiring to its level of prosperity and openness." [10] Soft power is making people *want* to do what you want them to do, which is fundamental to the idea of branding, and fundamental to the idea of America.

After a violent first century, America was determined to become the world's first soft-power empire and build its dominions entirely by trade and by brand. But in the second decade of the twentieth century, further violence and entanglement in other nations' disputes were to prove unavoidable.

3

Persuade or Perish: Brandishing Brand America

"I am not particularly concerned whether either gunpowder or propaganda have benefited or harmed mankind. I merely emphasize, at this point, that propaganda on an immense scale is here to stay. We Americans must become informed and adept at its use, defensively and offensively, or we may find ourselves as archaic as the belted knight who refused to take gunpowder seriously 500 years ago."

George V. Allen, assistant secretary of state for public affairs, in a 1949 article "Propaganda: A conscious weapon of diplomacy"

Whom do you represent?

The idea of public diplomacy – that governments need to represent their countries to foreign publics and not only to other governments – is usually considered to date from the mid-twentieth century, and is seen as a typical product of the media age. The term itself is a modern one, and an American invention: a study prepared for the Senate Foreign Relations Committee by the Library of Congress mentions that it was first used by Dean Edmund Gullion of the Fletcher School of Law and Diplomacy at Tufts University in 1965.

Most foreign services also see public diplomacy as a recent arrival. It's a disturbing one too for old-school diplomats, as it means that these highly-trained elites need to learn a whole set of unfamiliar (and, to many, distasteful) new skills such as public relations, news conferences, media management, broadcast and interview techniques, and the ability to produce media-friendly soundbites at will.

Jan Melissen of the Dutch foreign policy think tank Clingendael uses the famous 1945 photograph of Roosevelt, Stalin and Churchill at the Yalta conference to illustrate how diplomacy has changed since the Second World War. All three leaders travelled slowly and privately by steamer to Yalta, where they sorted out the reconstruction of Europe and the new world order. Having done this, they sailed slowly back to their countries, after which the public was duly informed of their decisions. Melissen contrasts this staid and exclusive affair with twenty-first-century summits such as Geneva, Genoa and Seattle, which dominate the world's TV screens for days on end, and where you can't move for journalists and protesters. Instant communications and widespread democracy are squeezing out old-fashioned private diplomacy: like it or not, international relations now take place in real time, before a global audience.

The nervousness of some diplomats is understandable, but in fact they had plenty of warning about the way diplomacy was heading. The first stirrings of a more public and more liberal-democratic approach to international relations took place in America nearly two centuries before Yalta.

In a 2003 speech on "Regaining America's Voice Overseas," Ed Feulner, president of the Heritage Foundation think tank and a former chairman of the US Advisory Commission on Public Diplomacy, observed: "Historians might trace the beginnings of American public diplomacy to World War II and the establishment of the Voice of America to counter propaganda from German and Japanese enemy radio broadcasts ... [but] even before World War II, Americans proved that we have always been good at advocating our own cause," and he went on to mention Franklin, who, as we have seen in the previous chapter, was a great and very public diplomat.

Similarly, in the anthology *The Great Republic by the Master Historians,* editor Hubert H. Bancroft quotes "a French historian of the first celebrity" describing Franklin's masterful representation not only of America's interests, but of the American ideal. It all sounds very close to the modern idea of public diplomacy:

> By the effect which Franklin produced in France, one might say that he fulfilled his mission, not with a court, but with a free people. Diplomatic etiquette did not permit him often to hold interviews with the ministers, but he associated with all the distinguished personages who directed public opinion.

In marketing terms, Franklin was targeting opinion formers, that sector just below the official elite whose high position and reputation mean that their tastes, views and ideas are at the vanguard of widespread popularity. Clearly, they're an important audience to identify and influence, and this is a good example of the mass communication skills that modern diplomats are now having to acquire.

Franklin and his successors deliberately moulded the American diplomatic style as an expression of American identity. "Americans, from the earliest days of independence, have consciously sought to avoid European diplomatic models," says Monteagle Stearns. "We have seen ourselves, rightly or wrongly, as practitioners of a new diplomacy, born of the Enlightenment, in which the power of reason would replace military power and distinctions between personal and state morality would be narrowed if not entirely eliminated." [11]

Public diplomacy is now recognized as a vital component of nation branding. In fact, the two terms are often used interchangeably, partly because the State Department is in charge of marketing the nation. But using the term in this context is confusing because it also has a more precise meaning – the public communication of *government policy* – that is only one point of the hexagon, not the whole thing.

These days, there is more collaboration and integration between embassies, cultural bodies and trade and tourist offices, and modern diplomats see promoting trade, tourism, investment and culture as an important part of their job. But countries generally get the biggest improvement in their overall brand image when all the points of the hexagon are aligned with a common strategy. The ministry of foreign affairs may or may not be the right body to lead this process, but whatever the administrative structure, it's clear that all the major stakeholders of the country's image need to be fully represented on it.

"Brand" is a good word to use when talking about countries because it's the only one that truly conveys the idea of a deliberate *capture* and *accumulation* of reputational value. Ordinary promotion, when it's carried out with no particular long-term national strategy in mind apart from growth, is an endless cycle that may or may not lead to economic development in the longer term. Unlike branding, it's about *selling* the country to companies and investors: selling holidays to tourists, selling the government's policies to voters and the media and foreign publics, selling culture, selling heritage, and so on. It can be effective, but unless it's directed and driven by an underlying brand strategy, there is little chance that the country as a whole will acquire what marketing professor David A. Aaker called *brand equity*.

Every act of promotion, exchange or representation needs to be seen not as an end in itself but as an opportunity to build the country's overall reputation. America seems to have instinctively understood, centuries before most other countries, that the growth, management and protection of its good name – its brand – are the real and valuable purpose behind its daily acts of international engagement.

The term "public diplomacy" is closer in meaning to nation branding if the word "public" is applied to the messenger as well as the audience; in other words, when the entire population is motivated and energized through a benign national ambition, and instinctively seizes every opportunity to tell the world about their country. If traditional diplomacy is government-to-government (G2G) and public diplomacy is government-to-people (G2P), then effective nation branding also includes an element of P2P. Some countries, such as Italy and America, seem to achieve the P2P spirit quite naturally, while others, such as Britain and Germany, find it much more of a problem.

He wants you

"There is no other country in the world," argues American propaganda scholar Nancy Snow, "that matches ours for developing such close links between commerce (salesmanship) and the business of government (statesmanship)... The United States has a one-hundred-year history of marrying commerce with politics and tapping public relations to 'brand' America abroad. President Woodrow Wilson told the International Congress of Salesmanship to 'go out and sell goods that will make the world more comfortable and more happy and convert them to the principles of America.' That was in 1916." [12]

With America on the verge of entering the war in Europe, those would not be Wilson's last words on the subject of selling Brand America. After running for re-election in 1916 with the slogan "He kept us out of war," Woodrow Wilson faced a dilemma when, in 1917, he decided to lead America to war after all.

Germany had resumed its submarine attacks on passenger and freight liners, and torpedoed the *Lusitania* in 1915, killing 128 Americans and more than a thousand others. Word also got out that the Germans were urging Mexico to invade Texas and New Mexico. These were sufficient reasons to go to war for Wilson and for Congress, but not necessarily for the American people, even though anti-German feelings were strong. Support for the war still had to be built, and morale needed to be maintained.

So, on 13 April 1917, seven days after America entered the war, Wilson inaugurated the Committee on Public Information, appointing his friend George Creel, a former boxer and police chief, to lead it. At the time of his appointment, Creel was a muck-raking journalist and editor of the *Rocky Mountain News* in Colorado. His aim was straightforward and ambitious. "What we had to have," wrote Creel in his 1920 memoir *How We Advertised*

Swim Ink/CORBIS

America, "was no mere surface unity, but a passionate belief in the justice of America's cause that should weld the people of the United States into one white-hot mass."

The staple of the CPI's arsenal was news releases sent to news outlets, which used them to fill regular columns. Realizing that many readers skipped past the front pages of the paper and headed straight for the features section, the CPI's Division of Syndicated Features recruited the leading novelists, essayists and short-story writers of the day. According to a later account, "These popular American writers presented the official line in an easily digestible form, and their work was said to have reached 12 million people every month."[13]

Meanwhile, the CPI's Division of Pictorial Publicity, headed by the illustrator Charles Dana Gibson, produced one of the most famous propaganda images ever: the finger-pointing Uncle Sam "I want you" recruitment poster, illustrated by James Montgomery Flagg. Slogans were developed too. Two that have since become clichés and are usually used ironically were originally popularized by the Creel committee: "The war to end war" and "Making the world safe for democracy."

Perhaps the most inventive Creel effort was The 4-Minute Men, a body of 75,000 citizen volunteers who delivered short speeches in cinemas and other public places encouraging their fellow countrymen to buy war bonds, donate to the Red Cross and enlist in the army. They spoke for the four minutes it took to change a reel, and the name is also a patriotic reference to the Minute Men, the volunteer colonial militia (no more than armed and very brave farmers, really) who fought the British at Lexington and Concord in the opening skirmishes of the Revolutionary War. Committee records say that in less than two years before the war ended in 1918, some 7,555,190 speeches were made, "every one," said Creel the wordsmith, "having the carry of shrapnel."[14]

The development from Minute Men to 4-Minute Men shows

how America had changed, and the world around it, between the eighteenth and the twentieth century. Wars hadn't ceased, or become any less bloody, but the importance of influencing the public, at home and abroad, had become a primary preoccupation, and a recognized weapon of war.

The spirit of radio

"The domestic task was simple," wrote Creel after the war, "compared with the undertaking that faced the Committee when it turned from the United States to wage the battle for world opinion. It was not only that the people of the Allied Powers had to be strengthened with a message of encouragement, but there was also the moral verdict of the neutral nations to be won and the stubborn problem of reaching the deluded soldiers and civilians of the Central Powers with the truths of the war." [15]

Radio was the answer. Not as a way to broadcast directly to millions of listeners – at least not yet – but for transmitting the American version of the news to journalists across the globe. Using chains of relay stations in friendly nations (or, failing this, using antennae mounted on navy ships), the committee distributed its news releases from France to the Philippines, Scandinavia to Siberia. News services as far away as Australia were able to pluck the signal from the air in the evening and run the stories in the next day's papers.

Reminiscing in a 1922 article called "The battle in the air lanes," Creel observed that "it was in recognition of Public Opinion as a major force that the Great War differed most essentially from all previous conflicts." Like his counterparts before and after, he saw his task in moral terms: "The trial of strength was not only between massed bodies of armed men, but between opposed ideals, and moral verdicts took on all the value of

CORBIS

"The world's greatest adventure in advertising" is how Creel described his committee's campaign.

military decisions ... in all things, from first to last, without halt. Other wars went no deeper than the physical aspects, but German Kultur raised issues that had to be fought out in the hearts and minds of people as well as on the actual firing-line. This was the fight that the Committee on Public Information was called upon to make."

The CPI's work was another in a long line of America's efforts to justify itself to the world since the Declaration of Independence in 1776. Just like the Founding Fathers, Creel was in his own words seeking "the verdict of mankind" in pleading "the justice of America's cause before the jury of Public Opinion."

Creel saw his task as spreading the truth: no more, no less. As he put it, "Our effort was educational and informative throughout, for we had such confidence in our case as to feel that no other argument was needed than the simple, straightforward presentation of facts."

Few modern marketers would agree with Creel on this point, or believe that he really meant it. It is a principle of marketing – some call it cynical, others realistic – that there is no such thing as a truth so forceful that it sweeps away all doubts and objections. Even if there were, say the more hard-bitten marketers, most people wouldn't recognize it if they saw it. The truth, however truthful, never sells itself: it has to be *sold.*

This is not because we are intellectually or morally incapable of making up our own minds about the truth. Most of the time, we just can't be bothered, especially if it comes to us through a medium in which we are used to having some editorial comment. Getting political facts from the radio or a newspaper without a trace of commentary is like buying a tub of ice cream at the cinema and discovering once you get back to your seat and the lights go down that they've forgotten to pack the little spoon with it.

At any rate, the Committee on Public Information's broadcasting operation was the progenitor of the ones that the US keeps active today – Voice of America, Radio Free Europe, Radio Liberty, Radio and TV Marti, Radio Free Asia, Worldnet Television and Radio Sawa in the Middle East – which together reach some 100 million people weekly in 65 languages. Anyone who believes in the value of these services owes a debt to that exuberant prize-fighter George Creel.

Is it or isn't it?

Many commentators have used the word "propaganda" to describe the CPI's work. Edward Bernays, the "father of PR," a nephew of Sigmund Freud and a member of Creel's committee, was more specific: "It was propaganda," he wrote, "not impropaganda." [16]

In those days, propaganda wasn't considered a negative word: it didn't imply manipulation and wasn't linked only with totalitarian regimes. As Barry Fulton, director of the Public Diplomacy Institute at George Washington University and a former US Information Agency official, puts it: "Until the mid-60s, if somebody called you a propagandist, nobody was offended. Later on it begins to have a tone of doing something underhanded." [17]

It is difficult to discuss public diplomacy or the branding of countries without morality coming into the debate, which raises philosophical questions about reality and perception. The moralist's view is that only reality creates perceptions, and any attempt to shortcut this process by tampering directly with people's perceptions amounts to distortion, the act of a dishonest government. Moralists think it is shallow for policy makers to be concerned with public opinion, and indicates flawed motivations. Governments, they say, should concentrate on substantive things rather than frittering away time and money in some vain pursuit of public approval.

There are several problems with this argument. It might be true that if people knew all the facts about an issue, and every argument for and against it, then they could understand it completely and develop the "right" response. But most issues are too complex for simple answers, and they often involve specialist or technical knowledge that most people don't have. And few of us have the time or the inclination to ponder matters of public policy or international affairs; we usually say it's not our job, and that's why we have a government. So governments (and the media) usually present an abbreviated version of the facts, and sometimes it's an approximately fair representation of both sides of the argument, and sometimes it's a very loaded form of partial truthfulness. Most of the time nobody knows because it's too difficult to work it out, so we fall back on trusting our governments and the media. And which government and which media we trust depends very much on the power of their brands.

As we have seen, it is hard to separate reality from perception, and the distinction is often more academic than practical. In politics and in commerce, our perceptions of companies and policies are what really count, because they are what drive our behaviour. It therefore makes perfect sense for governments to take the *perceptual implications* of their policies very seriously indeed. The question "How is this going to look?" shows more than vanity – it shows an understanding of human nature.

Any attempt to manage or manipulate public perceptions directly, without regard to the actions that create the perceptions, may rightly be viewed with suspicion, and in fact sounds like a reasonable definition of propaganda. But even here it's not a simple matter, because we can't assume that people's perceptions are always fair, or that they are always the simple consequence of exposure to the truth. Our perceptions of countries are, in fact, almost never fair; they are made of clichés, half-truths, outdated commonplaces, prejudice and ignorance. So who decides whether trying to "correct" a perception so that it "correctly" reflects reality is legitimate place branding or "propaganda – not impropaganda"?

It is certainly right that you have to *earn* your reputation, not construct it. But it seems perfectly legitimate, in fact essential, to take the trouble to look after it.

A country can behave impeccably for decades and yet still be saddled with a bad reputation that was formed long ago, and may not have been fair even then. Indeed, this is quite common. National images take a long time to form; they are made out of clichés and prejudices that sometimes seem *rusted* into place. It's like starlight, which by the time it reaches us on earth is only the distant echo of an event that started and ended long before. In such cases it is obvious that the country's impeccable behaviour simply isn't being noticed, and can't be depended on to shift the negative perception. Surely the government of such a country is justified in trying to act directly on its reputation, and surely you can't call that propaganda. But who decides when the case isn't so clear-cut?

When people use terms like public diplomacy, they are partly doing so to reassure people that this is something quite different from propaganda. Hans Tuch, a retired minister in the US Foreign Service, says, "I define public diplomacy as a government's process of communicating with foreign publics in an attempt to bring about understanding for its nation's ideas and ideals, its institutions and culture, as well as its national goals and current policies." [18]

So public diplomacy is about being understood in a helpful way – which sounds not just ethically proper, but positively enlightened. But think about that phrase "bring about understanding." There's a world of implication in that carefully selected phrase. And the modest use of the word "attempt" is telling: in other words, success is not guaranteed, which is very reassuring. Any suggestion of coercion has been carefully removed from the sentence.

Vocabulary is important in making the case for public diplomacy. There is definitely something inflammatory about the language of marketing. Marketers have long been in the habit of talking cavalierly about the techniques of persuasion, coldly classifying people into consumer "types," controlling the "drivers of behaviour," and so on. If you're not used to it, it's a vocabulary that sounds cynical, arrogant, even sinister, and politicians would do well not to imitate it too closely, now matter how modern they may think it makes them sound.

But the simple fact is that it's enormously difficult to make people change their minds, let alone their behaviour. In the end, it's not the law or the morality of politicians that protects citizens from propaganda, but the fact that they probably couldn't do it if they tried, especially to a well-educated population in a modern democracy.

The influence of marketing on governance is probably a benign one for this reason, and it seems more likely to teach politicians humility than encourage tyranny. There are few better ways of learning about the intractability of human nature than spending several years of your life trying to persuade people to spend their hard-earned cash on one brand rather than another. Indeed, there's something inherently democratic about a marketing approach to public affairs, because it's about persuasion rather than coercion, and it's a fair contest between the politicians and the public (with the media and other commentators helping out). It depends heavily on rhetoric, which has always been an integral part of the democratic approach to public matters, and which is one of the main tools of marketing.

Marketing teaches that truthfulness makes sound practical and commercial sense: you can only lie once. Edward R. Murrow, the legendary newsman and later one of the outstanding figures of American public diplomacy, saw the truth not only as a powerful weapon, but as an intrinsic trait of Brand America: "American traditions and the American ethic require us to be truthful, but the most important reason is that truth is the best propaganda and lies are the worst. To be persuasive we must be believable; to be believable we must be credible; to be credible we must be truthful. It is as simple as that." [19]

The weapons proliferate

American domestic morale was once again a critical factor after the outbreak of World War II. President Roosevelt, himself a clever manager of the press, realized there was a need for an agency to explain defence preparations to the public, and so in September 1939 he created the Office of Government Reports.

Once the United States entered the war, communication became even more vital. In Clayton Laurie's recent estimation, Creel's committee had been "simplistic, heavily nationalistic and ultrapatriotic, and prone to hysterical, lurid, and crude exaggeration." Therefore, says Laurie, "the CPI became the model for the sort of agency that Roosevelt sought to avoid."

But Roosevelt knew he had to do something to counter Nazi propaganda at home as well as overseas. In July 1941, he issued an executive order creating the Office of the Coordinator of Information (COI). He designated William J. "Wild Bill" Donovan its director. This accomplished and staunchly conservative Republican had been a World War I combat hero, a politician (he served under President Coolidge as a deputy Attorney General and ran unsuccessfully for governor of New York) and a Wall Street lawyer. Although he could make $500,000 a year as an attorney, he didn't care for personal wealth. His passion was for world affairs and travel, which he conducted at the highest level; in 1935, on a trip to Rome, he discussed the war in Ethiopia with Benito Mussolini. Donovan also had an abiding interest in intelligence and morale matters.

In the months that followed the establishment of the COI, a handful of other "alphabet agencies" with missions related to propaganda proliferated at Roosevelt's behest. On 13 June 1942, the whole lot – the COI and the OGR, along with departments called the FIS and the OFF – were regrouped and relaunched as the OSS (Office of Strategic Services), commanded by Bill Donovan, and the OWI (Office of War Information).

The OWI, headed by popular broadcast journalist and former *New York Times* editorial writer Elmer Davis, would soon become one of the largest propaganda organizations ever created. It's not clear, however, that Davis himself saw it that way. James P. Warburg, one of Davis' deputies at OWI (and a noted banker whose firm merged decades later with the Union Bank of Switzerland to form UBS Warburg), believed the "purpose of spreading information is to promote the functioning of man's reason [and] the purpose of propaganda is to mobilize certain of man's emotions in such a way that they will dominate his reason." According to Warburg, Davis wanted the OWI to be a "high class international news service [and didn't] understand that he was being entrusted with the management of an important branch of modern warfare."

Between these two men raged, once again, the battle between the "inform" school and the "persuade" school. Davis himself felt that "America should tell the truth, tell it intelligently, and tell it everywhere." The object of the OWI, in his view, was to "educate...listeners in a true interpretation of the enemy's designs, create a distrust of the enemy, and diminish their prestige." Operating at the business end of this notion was Robert Sherwood, a playwright and friend of the president's, who oversaw the overseas branch of the OWI in accordance with

Walker Evans/Smithsonian Institute/Gift of Sheldon-Claire Company

This WWII poster aimed to inspire strong internal support for the brand.

his view that America's values "constitute one ideology that men of freedom and goodwill can turn to."

Whatever the news, the OWI gave a truthful story, but perhaps not what we would call a straight story. It attempted routinely, in the words of its bosses, to "create a picture of absolutely overwhelming" military might on the Allied side and "to heighten the feeling of doom and collapse which is in store for Germany."

But while the OWI always painted the gloomiest picture of the Axis situation, it did so using careful emphasis rather than lies. In fact, says Laurie, "the agency's propaganda became more sober and factual as the war progressed." Allied mistakes and setbacks "were treated cautiously but not pessimistically" by OWI; in keeping with the agency's policy of truthfulness, they were never glossed over entirely. And a glimmer of hope was usually extended to Germans by means of explanations that surrender would mean not annihilation, as Nazi propagandists claimed, but rather, in OWI's words, "peace and an opportunity for all nations, large and small, to take part ultimately in a better world."

Rumours of lonely women

With the OWI handling overt official propaganda and information dissemination, Donovan now had licence to use his OSS to create a more subversive variety that he believed was essential and which, he complained, he "had not been able to develop in the old COI, where the adepts of black propaganda were badly outnumbered by the 'truth-will-win-out' believers.'" [20] The Office of Strategic Services thus became America's first non-military intelligence agency. Its agenda was to demoralize the Wehrmacht and undermine the faith of German citizens and soldiers in their cause – to convey, in other words, that defeat was not only imminent, but, because the American way was better, also in Germany's best interest.

The Morale Operations (MO) division of the OSS directed covert strategic and tactical operations based on deception and subversion. Because MO output was unofficial and disclaimed by federal authorities, it could act without fear of damaging the OWI's efforts or America's reputation in general.

One of its favourite techniques in its early days was the spreading of rumours painstakingly created to appear of homegrown enemy origin. Up to 20 rumours were thought up and dispersed each week, and "consisted of simple, brief, concrete, and vivid stories, purporting to come from inside sources concerning familiar persons and events... [They] were intended to subvert and deceive, to promote fear, anxiety, confusion, overconfidence, distrust and panic." Just like many good advertisements, successful rumours "were easy to remember, had a plot, concerned current events, and appealed to emotion and sentiment." Success was measured by the "comeback" – the number of mentions of the rumour in Axis or Allied press or neutral media – just as you would evaluate a PR campaign today.

For example, MO rumours in June 1944 "included stories that British paratroopers had landed in Berlin, German sailors in Wilhelmshaven had shot their officers, Field Marshals Rommel and von Rundstedt had been captured, Luftwaffe pilots were refusing to fly, foreign workers had taken over the Krupp factory in Essen, former Nazi leader Rudolf Hess was leading a detachment of Allied troops in France, and Wehrmacht rations had been found to have been poisoned." These stories must have had a considerable impact on enemy morale, and made an important contribution to the war effort. If even a few of them managed to achieve regular dissemination and spread to a significant proportion of the enemy's troops, their effect on a large group of frightened, disorientated young men must have been pretty potent.

Imagine the effect of such an operation in a commercial environment. The damage to *esprit de corps* and consequently to productivity, customer service, staff retention, discipline and quality control could be devastating, and one wonders whether such tactics have ever been used by one company to cripple another. Military units are yet another example of how groups of human beings tend to think and behave according to certain patterns, and how certain techniques can disrupt or affect this process in more or less predictable ways. This is why marketing is bound to find itself chatting over the fence with politicians and soldiers, because they all have the same basic aims and the same basic challenges.

The League of Lonely German Women, one of MO's most inventive and insidious plots, played heavily on the anxieties of German soldiers. A heart-shaped MO-created lapel pin was distributed – heaven only knows how – to German troops. It was accompanied by a leaflet explaining that the pin, which was to be worn while on leave, would identify the wearer to members of the league: lonely German women eager to do their bit for the war through sexual promiscuity. "Don't be shy," the instructions urged. "Your wife, sister, and sweetheart is one of us. We think of you, but we also think of Germany." The comeback was extraordinary, with press mentions as far afield as *Time* magazine and the *Canadian Tribune*. Both pin and leaflet were discovered in the possession of many captured German soldiers.

This is one of the earliest examples of what one might call *belligerent branding* on the part of the United States, where the instruments of publicity are deliberately used to damage the internal or external identity and reputation of an enemy. As we shall see later, belligerent branding was eventually to become a permanent feature of American branding operations.

People often comment on the fact that the vocabulary of marketing is full of metaphors borrowed from warfare: campaign, target, strategy, marketing offensive and so on. With the OSS, there was nothing metaphorical about it: this *was* warfare.

35mm ammunition

"They haven't the slightest enthusiasm for this war or this cause," newspaper editor William Allen told White House adviser Lowell Mellett about new army draftees in September 1940. "They are not grouchy, they are not mutinous, they just don't give a tinker's damn." [21] General George Marshall also reported that the new army morale branch was failing in its job because of the "deadly effects of prepared lectures indifferently read to bored troops." How could the US win a war Americans were too bored to support, let alone fight. Something needed to be done (and Pearl Harbor was not what America had in mind).

A step forward was taken when Major Frank Capra was assigned to the army's morale branch in February 1942, and ordered by General Marshall to "make a series of documented, factual-information films – the first in our history – that will explain to our boys in the Army why we are fighting, and the principles for which we are fighting." This was a stroke of genius on Marshall's part. Capra, an Italian immigrant, had already made such well-known Hollywood films as *Mr Smith Goes to Washington* (1939) starring Jimmy Stewart, and would go on to direct the classic *It's a Wonderful Life* (1946).

The splendid result was *Why We Fight,* a series of seven films starting with *A Prelude to War* (1943) and concluding with *Know Your Enemy: Japan* (1945). These motion pictures not only fulfilled their original military purpose, but were widely considered an advance in the art of documentary film making. The series garnered a New York Film Critics award and was shown in public movie houses by popular demand. Winston Churchill and the

Soviet government also ordered prints of their own.

Another notable propaganda film series from the era is the set of animated shorts produced by Disney. Among these are *Commander Duck* (1944), in which Donald Duck is given the assignment to take out a Japanese airfield; *Out of the Frying Pan and into the Firing Line* (1942), in which Minnie Mouse learns that bacon grease can be recycled into glycerine for munitions; and *Der Fuehrer's Face* (1943), which was originally entitled *Donald Duck in Nutzi Land* and features Donald in the guise of a Third Reich factory worker who throws tomatoes at Hitler. (Perhaps the Disney's Corporation's decision in May 2004 not to distribute Michael Moore's *Fahrenheit 9/11* is an expression of a longstanding patriotic streak.)

The walls between marketing, entertainment, politics and the military, always somewhat permeable in the American culture, had truly been dismantled by this stage.

America founds its Voice

The prototype for fact-based public diplomacy in America was the Declaration of Independence with its litany of substantiated charges against George III, since in addition to being a communiqué to the king of England, it was also an open letter to the people of the world. In 1776, however, it was far more urgent that the king get the message than that foreign publics be swayed by it. In the early 1940s, it was the other way round, and there was only one way to reach masses of people.

From an office on Madison Avenue in New York, Voice of America radio (though it wasn't called that just yet) went on air 79 days after the Japanese attack on Pearl Harbor. Its programme director was Romanian-born John Houseman, an actor well known for collaborating with Orson Welles on the infamous

War of the Worlds broadcast, a radio play so realistic that millions believed they were hearing about an actual alien invasion. Houseman and his team had worked frantically for weeks to get the studio up and running and ready for live broadcasts.

Although it would soon be one of the OWI's premier services, VOA was a bold move for the United States. As Alan L. Heil, Jr explains in his recent history of the Voice: "America was the last major power to broadcast internationally. It was entering uncharted waters, finding its 'sea legs' on the world's airwaves. By 1942, the Soviet Union had been at it for two decades, Britain, a decade; and France and Germany, nearly a decade."

Announcer William Harlan Hale, a banker and author who spoke German with only a slight American accent, was chosen to do the first broadcast, set for 2.30 a.m. on 25 February 1942 – prime morning time in occupied Europe. He told the tale afterwards:

> By a strange irony, it so happened that before the broadcast, I had an invitation to dinner and a ballet and I was dressed accordingly for the occasion.... It was the last ballet I saw during the war, but it was a strange affair to appear before the microphone speaking to the enemy fully dressed....Some BBC people who were in the studio thought that we let them down. They said: "You didn't tell us that this was a black tie affair."

At the appointed time, Hale stepped up to the mike and spoke: "We bring you Voice from America. Today, and daily from now on, we shall speak to you about America and the war. The news may be good for us. The news may be bad. But we shall tell you the truth."

"We went on the air," Houseman recalled, "with no name, out

of a cramped studio, on borrowed transmitters, with absolutely no direction from anyone as to what we should broadcast other than the truth."[22]

But the VOA News Branch stylebook, entitled *This Is Your Job,* made it clear that truth was a means to an end: "We are not in the business to amuse, entertain or simply inform our listeners. Nor are we in the business because news is an end itself. The United States is in the midst of a serious struggle for the mind of mankind and the only purpose of the News Branch as well as the entire Voice of America is to contribute toward winning that struggle."

Indeed, the VOA, as a subsidiary of the Office of War Information, was more than capable of selling the Brand of the Free. Here is Clayton Laurie (quoting in places from Holly Shulman's *Voice of Victory*):

> Nearly every OWI directive of the period contained a section "Projection of America."... In one early VOA program series, "United America Fights," beamed to friends and foes alike, the OWI portrayed the United States as "a diverse country devoted to democracy, imbued with the principles of equality and dedicated to social mobility." Accordingly, "the scripts read like a textbook on the great principles of American ideology and mythology." Post-war goals were a staple of the broadcasts rather than more immediate wartime tactical goals and were put "in aggressively democratic terms – ridding the world of oppression and tyranny and giving the world peace and freedom."

Then at long last, in 1945, victory: VE day in May, VJ day in August. On 25 August 1945, President Truman signed executive order 9608 abolishing the OWI. The Voice of America was placed temporarily in the State Department, pending a final decision on its fate. In 1947, Donovan's OSS would become the Central Intelligence Agency.

And public diplomacy had earned its stripes in warfare, once and for all. Now it had only to earn them in peacetime.

4

To Know Us is to Love Us: The Guerilla Marketing of Brand America

"Democracy is a fire in the minds of men. That fire depends on constant communication back and forth, a sharing of information, ideas, skills, experience."

James Billington, former Librarian of Congress

Great expectations

Americans always think they're the good guys. Because they take it as self-evident that their country's motives are pure and its polices, values and way of life essentially sound, they tend to blame miscommunication when American popularity suffers. "It can't be anything we're doing that's upsetting people," the logic seems to run, "so we must be being misunderstood."

This faith in communications as the way to project American values was evident at least as far back as the Creel days, and became almost unshakeable during the Cold War. This is partly because the Cold War was so much a war of ideas and values, in which America really did seem by any reasonable standards to be in the right.

And it's not hard to see why America, the home of brands and the freedom to shop, found the Soviet Union such an unappealing, even repellent prospect. A brand-free zone where people had to be citizens rather than consumers and were fed politics and ideology rather than entertainment, where shopping was a misery, where there was no choice, no opportunities for enrichment and no leisure – the USSR was America in looking-glass land.

In addition to being an ideological war, the Cold War had many tangible manifestations as the West, led by America, did its best to keep the red areas on the map from spreading. To fight the tangible war, America chose to engage in a number of actions that didn't quite match up to its values. It supported some pretty bad characters, engaged in some unsavoury covert operations and meddled promiscuously in the affairs of countries far from home.

Arguably, these are the actions that have started to produce what Chalmers Johnson calls "blowback": the unintended consequences of American foreign policy. What consumer backlash is to a brand, blowback is to a nation: when the disconnect between the brand message and corporate behaviour becomes too great, the marketing too hypocritical, the end justifying the means a little too often, then public protest tends to be intense in proportion to the strength of the brand. This is because a brand, as the clear, highly visible public manifestation of a country or corporation, is as much an invitation to complain – indeed, a target for grudges – as it is a guarantee of quality or a licence for its owner to sell more stuff. The higher you raise people's expectations with a brand, and the more you invest in making big public promises, the greater the disappointment when you fail to keep them.

The truth campaign

In April 1950, President Truman addressed the American Society of Newspaper Editors in what would become known as the "Campaign of Truth" speech:

> The cause of freedom is being challenged throughout the world today by the forces of imperialistic communism. This is a struggle, above all else, for the minds of men. Propaganda is one of the most powerful weapons the communists have in this struggle. Deceit, distortion, and lies are systematically used by them as a matter of deliberate policy.
>
> The propaganda can be overcome by truth – plain, simple, unvarnished truth – presented by newspapers, radio, newsreels, and other sources that the people trust....

> We know how false these communist promises are. But it is not enough for us to know this. Unless we get the real story across to people in other countries, we will lose the battle for men's minds by pure default....
>
> We must make ourselves known as we really are – not as communist propaganda pictures us. We must pool our efforts with those of other free people in a sustained, intensified program to promote the cause of freedom against the propaganda of slavery. We must make ourselves heard round the world in a great campaign of truth.

The mechanism for making America heard was public diplomacy, described by *Washington Post* columnist Jim Hoagland as "the euphemism for that...black art, national propaganda promotion." But again, whatever you call it, Hoagland says "the VoA and other propaganda outlets were important instruments in winning the Cold War. Soviet and East European citizens were given an easily assimilated message: 'Your government is lying to you. It is lying about your conditions in life, about itself, and most of all about the West.'" [23]

Oddly, Congress was sufficiently uncomfortable with the truthfulness of the truth that America developed for the rest of the world that in 1948 it passed the Smith-Mundt Act, making it illegal to distribute international propaganda domestically. The original intent of Smith-Mundt, says Nancy Snow, "was to protect the American public from propaganda techniques designed to influence ambivalent overseas publics or campaigns targeting enemies of the US." [24]

As a consequence of this law, however, few Americans know much about the instruments of their nation's public diplomacy –

the great institutions like Voice of America – or realize how effective and influential they have been. It's a curious notion that American propaganda should be considered too virulent for its own population to be safely exposed to it, as if the snake was afraid of its own bite.

Smith-Mundt certainly shows how seriously public diplomacy was taken as an offensive weapon. But keeping people in the dark about what you're doing overseas is a highly risky strategy for a government, since it breaks that vital connection between the ordinary people and what its elected representatives are telling the world about them.

A recent case in the commercial sector shows the danger of taking this approach. A big consulting firm decided to run an advertising campaign featuring its motivated, highly qualified workforce, but the marketing department didn't think it necessary to tell the staff about the campaign beforehand, and found it easier to make up the quotes and use professional models instead of photographing real employees. When the staff eventually saw themselves falsely represented by their own management in the campaign, they felt a keen sense of insult and betrayal, and the ads had to be withdrawn.

The point of the nation-branding hexagon marked "people" is the hardest yet the most important one for countries to build into their plans. It should *never* be disconnected from the other points of the hexagon, for the simple reason that if the brand isn't understood, shared, supported and reflected in the values and behaviours of the people, there is almost no chance that the brand strategy will ever be fulfilled. The people – the "human capital" – are after all the nation's principal asset.

If a nation sells itself as warm and welcoming, but its citizens tend to treat visitors with distrust (or perhaps it's just in their culture to be a bit reserved), those visitors will feel that they've been lied to, and the nation's reputation will fall further than if no promises had been made in the first place – at least in their opinion, and in the opinion of all the friends and relatives they discuss it with.

The idea of nation branding, like any kind of statecraft, is ethically and politically neutral: it can be used as an instrument of democratic progress or as one of manipulation and deceit. Failing to engage the population in the project is the first step from the former to the latter.

As more than one commentator on country branding has pointed out, one big difference between selling a tin of beans and selling a country is that you don't need to ask the beans what you put on the label.

Reorienting the former enemy

Smith-Mundt was, in its own words, "an act to promote the better understanding of the United States among the peoples of the world and to strengthen cooperative international relations," and it specified that the State Department would coordinate all public diplomacy and overseas information functions of the United States. This held until 1953, when all such functions were transferred to the newly established US Information Agency (then known as the US Information Service Abroad). Although the USIA's objective was to convey information, its policies and programmes ran along two tracks: one an anti-communist Cold War track, the other a programme of cultural activities that began with the occupation of Japan, Germany and Austria.

Diplomat Hans Tuch recalls in his book *Communicating with the World* that "the tone of USIA's output was at times propagandistic and simplistic, reflecting the techniques of American advertising.... USIA's first director came from the advertising industry... and gave scant attention to whether and how the American message might be received by audiences abroad. Selling 'People's Capitalism' became the slogan labeling the agency's promotional task, with little regard to how the term 'capitalism' might strike peoples living in other societies."

Insufficient understanding of the different ways that foreign publics interpret American ideas has often bedevilled American policy and commerce overseas. Americans tend to believe that their ideals are universal, and are surprised to discover that foreigners either don't understand exactly what they mean by democracy, freedom, quality, ambition, individualism, passion or commitment, or else they do understand but simply don't invest these ideals with the same importance. In fact, some of the concepts at the heart of American ideology, commerce and culture don't translate well into other cultures. Democracy itself is a tough sell in what anthropologists call "high power distance" cultures, such as Middle Eastern countries, where people make a different pact with authority, self-determination can be an alarming prospect, and rule by the many looks not unlike anarchy.

Americans have a habit of mistaking America for the world, and so lose out on many opportunities to present their case to important overseas audiences far faster, more simply, more accurately and more successfully, just because they haven't appreciated the need to *translate.* It's another aspect of the error of US public diplomacy that merely presenting the "unvarnished truth" about America is enough to win over people's hearts and minds; America has often believed that export is the key to expansion. Just send the stuff over – whether it's the best American literature through the USIA, or the best American popular culture through the movies, or the best American products – and people will be grateful.

Ideas of *exchange,* of true marketing (fully understanding the consumer long before you decide what he or she actually wants), and of true branding (creating a two-way relationship with the consumer), are not all that frequent in the annals of American public diplomacy. This is odd, because these are techniques and approaches that were invented by American companies, as we saw earlier, although it's true they were developed in the context of the highly monocultural domestic marketplace. Even American companies, with their advanced understanding of consumer needs and of the two-way relationships that are fundamental to brand building, have often found it hard to practise what they preach when the consumer is not American. But they have managed it often enough to be able to teach American policy makers some valuable lessons.

"The other principal foundation stone of US public diplomacy," continues Tuch, "was the government's effort, in the years following the Allied victory, to reorient and re-educate the peoples of the defeated totalitarian nations of Nazi Germany, Austria and Japan toward democracy. These programs, between 1946 and 1954, involved the US government for the first time in extensive and long-range cultural, educational and social programs abroad. Activities concerned with cultural and education exchanges, publishing, libraries and cultural centers, secondary schools, universities, and social reforms were introduced and, in some cases, imposed, in order to bring to the peoples of these defeated nations a new democratic way of life and democratic institutions." [25] The basic idea, in the words of historian John Dower, was for the former enemies to "embrace defeat."

Each of these libraries, or "Amerika Hauser" as they were called in Germany, such as the one in Frankfurt in which Hans Tuch served early in his diplomatic career, had about 45,000 volumes, some 300 newspapers and magazines, and "a staff of some 45 librarians, programmers, artists, English teachers, and administrative personnel." Famous American authors such as Thornton Wilder came to lecture, and the Juilliard String Quartet came to perform. A German researcher wrote in 1984:

"The principal impact of the America Houses was...in influencing and changing the view of America among the German people. Through the medium of the library it was possible to persuade many Germans to regard America positively and often admiringly." [26]

Public diplomacy activity was not limited to Germany, Austria and Japan. "The [USIA] quickly thrived," wrote Wilson Dizard, Jr, a retired senior Foreign Service officer, in his article "Remembering USIA" on the fiftieth anniversary of the agency's founding. "Within a few years [it] had operations in over 270 cities and towns around the world, with the major expansion taking place in Asia and Latin America. This was a broader overseas presence than that of any other US government agency, then or since. The USIS post in Kathmandu predated the establishment of the embassy by five years. Similarly, USIA was operating in Kirkuk in northern Iraq well before State opened a consulate there. For many years, USIS posts were the sole American presence in scores of other cities, from Rajshahi, Bangladesh, to the Norwegian town of Tromsø, 200 miles north of the Arctic Circle."

And lest anyone think that protesting against America by defacing its foreign assets is a new phenomenon, here is Dizard's account of the experiences of American overseas libraries: "Most USIS posts were small, staffed by two or three officers (initially limited to Foreign Service Reserve status) together with local support staff. The posts' most prominent feature was usually a street-front library, which was often the first open-shelf lending library in the city. Available to all comers, the libraries were filled with students throughout the day. In Morocco, the traffic was so heavy that USIS issued library cards in seven colors, allowing borrowers entry only once a week. In Calcutta, students had to sign up in advance to assure a reading-room seat. Most libraries had large street-front windows which became convenient targets for political demonstrations by students and others. A *New Yorker* cartoon in the 1960s depicted a USIA training class where employees were being taught window glazing."

Getting to know us better

Senator William J. Fulbright, once described as a die-hard exponent of the "to know us is to love us school," believed that there was a limit to the power of long-distance communication. The challenge as he saw it, and as Edward R. Murrow would later express it, was to reach across "the last three feet" – the distance that separates two people who are talking to one another in the same room. To this end, Fulbright sponsored the Fulbright Act of 1946, so creating the Fulbright scholarship programme. This expanded the scope of cultural exchanges, recalls Dizard, to "encompass students, academics, media leaders and government officials, along with performing groups ranging from the New York Philharmonic to Appalachian square dancers."

These cultural exchanges have been one of the most enlightened components of America's public diplomacy efforts, and have resulted in some high-profile successes. According to Dizard, "In the early 1980s, the embassy in Kabul proposed a relatively unknown young journalist, Hamid Karzai, for a grant. It was a good hunch, given Karzai's later prominence as the interim president of Afghanistan following the overthrow of the Taliban regime. Other leader grantees included Britain's Tony Blair, ... Egypt's Anwar Sadat, and Tanzania's Julius Nyerere. During the USIA years, over 40 other leader grantees became heads of government or chiefs of state."

In 1967, as an up-and-coming member of parliament, Margaret Thatcher participated in the International Visitor Program. According to British scholar Giles Scot Smith, "The openness of the program, allowing remarkable freedom of access for the visitor to American social and political life, has definitely been one of its most valuable assets. Visitors expecting a propaganda exercise were pleasantly surprised to find it a very different experience." [27]

Fins and spin

"Chrome tail fins on new Cadillacs, bobby socks and Jell-O, Hula Hoops and Frigidaires, Chesterfields and food blenders, golf, Uncle Ike's grin, Mamie [Eisenhower]'s hats: welcome to the Nifty Fifties. This was the America of *Life* magazine," writes Frances Stonor Saunders. "But behind this was another America – brooding, dark, ill at ease" and worried about the threat of communism from within and without. [28]

One of the manifestations of the latter America was Fulbright's colleague Senator Joseph McCarthy and his deputies, lawyers Roy Cohn and David Schine. Hans Tuch was stationed in the USIA library in Frankfurt on the day Cohn paid a visit. Cohn, he recalls, was checking the library for communist influence, and objected strongly to the fact that it had a copy of Dashiell Hammett's *The Maltese Falcon* – not exactly a treatise on Marxism. In general, it was on this kind of flimsy "evidence" that McCarthy accused the USIA of harbouring communists among its staff.

"American cultural prestige was being ground underfoot," writes Saunders, "as government agencies and missions truckled to McCarthy. The average number of titles shipped abroad by USIA in 1953 plunged from 119,913 to 314.... Thoreau's essay on 'Civil Disobedience' was banned by the US at the same time as it was outlawed by Maoist China."

Adherence to any creed, whether it's the political ideologies of

Owaki-Kulla/CORBIS

a nation brand or the competitive philosophy of a commercial brand, can easily be taken to extremes. The need for consistent and coordinated behaviour on the part of every employee or citizen is so fundamental to the success of a venture that it's easy to fall into the trap of believing that any amount of coercion is justified in channelling people's thoughts and deeds into a narrower and narrower interpretation of the brand strategy. More than one CEO has done so, and generally not lasted very long.

It doesn't work, mercifully: you can force people to do most things, but you can't force them to be enthusiastic, and enthusiasm for a brand is the only way to sell it to an indifferent consumer. Avis, a company that has done more than most to create and maintain a powerful and cohesive internal brand, instituted the wise (and humane) rule that employees should always wear their "We try harder" badge, except once in a while when they woke up and just didn't feel like trying harder. On those days, went the rule, you should still come to work, just not wear the badge. Senator McCarthy evidently didn't have such days, and didn't see why anybody else should have them either.

Although Hans Tuch laments the prolonged effect that Senator McCarthy had on the morale of many public diplomacy professionals, McCarthy also had a more immediate impact: USIA and VOA staff felt unable to protest about the outrageously propagandistic materials that were sometimes produced. However, when George V. Allen (source of the gunpowder quote that heads chapter 3), took up the reins at USIA in 1957, he encouraged things to be played straight. An experienced diplomat, Allen had been US ambassador to India, Iran and Greece, and assistant Secretary of State for Near East and South Asian affairs. He had also been assistant Secretary of State for Public Affairs before the USIA was created, so he well understood the value of public diplomacy (although the term itself hadn't yet been coined).

"Allen also worked," says Tuch, "a major change of tone in the Voice of America. He [believed] VOA should strive to become an international broadcast medium, transmitting to the world comprehensive, accurate, and objective news.... His intent was to gain international acceptance for VOA as a respected source of information like the BBC ... [He insisted] that VOA, like the BBC, broadcast in English around the clock, in order to establish itself as a widely available, consistent, and authoritative voice."

The broadcaster formerly known as Egbert

As a university student at Washington State College, Egbert Roscoe Murrow followed the well-accepted American tradition of changing your own name, and rebranded himself as Edward. In 1935, he took a job at the Columbia Broadcasting System, where he rose rapidly through the ranks, becoming director of the CBS European office in London after just two years. His job was to solicit comments for CBS broadcasts from European officials and experts. At 29, he was CBS's only representative in Europe.

In 1939, with the help of a new hire, newspaper reporter William L. Shirer, Murrow made history by reporting the Nazi seizure of Austria and including in the broadcast reports from special correspondents in Berlin, London, Paris and Rome. As World War II got under way, Murrow carried on with similar broadcasts, beginning each with the words "This is London." He organized an eleven-member team of reporters, dubbed "Murrow's boys," whose reports from the major European capitals were heard on the CBS programme *World News Roundup.* Together, they established some of the core traditions of broadcast journalism.

According to a story broadcast recently on VOA in the easier-to-understand Special English:

> Murrow took his listeners places they had never been. He let them experience things they could not imagine. For example, after World War II, he was among the first Allied reporters to visit the Buchenwald prison camp operated by the Nazis in Germany during the war. This is how he described the prisoners there: "As we walked into the courtyard, a man fell dead. Two others, they must have been over 60, were crawling toward the latrine. I saw it, but will not describe it. In another part of the camp, they showed me the children, hundreds of them. Some were only six. One rolled up his sleeve and showed me his number. It was tattooed on his arm." [29]

Back in the US in 1946, Murrow was made vice-president of CBS News, but resigned the post a year later to return to broad-

Bettmann/CORBIS

Egbert goes to England.

casting. When television put an end to the golden age of radio in the 1950s, he switched to the new medium, developing several TV shows including one called *Person to Person,* in which he interviewed famous people in their homes. Guests included Eleanor Roosevelt (widow of FDR), Marilyn Monroe, Marlon Brando and Senator John F. Kennedy.

When Kennedy became president in 1961, he asked Murrow to take the helm at USIA. Murrow accepted. Not surprisingly, public diplomacy came naturally to him. He had a passion for the work, and a feel for it. "It has always seemed to me," he said, "the real art in this business is not so much moving information or guidance or policy five or ten thousand miles. That is an electronic problem. The real art is to move it the last three feet in face-to-face conversation." It pleased his subordinates no end that their boss regarded their work as an art. Murrow's direction, says Tuch, was "more spiritual, inspirational, and substantive than managerial."

It was also visionary, and wise. When he found out about the CIA's botched attempt to invade Cuba at the Bay of Pigs in April 1961, he was "spitting mad" according to the then VOA director Henry Loomis. "They expect us to be in on the crash landings," Murrow seethed down the line to Loomis. "We had better be in on the takeoffs [too]."

Kennedy apparently took this advice, for in January 1963 his administration issued the USIA with new orders. Its role would no longer be merely to inform and explain US objectives, but "to help achieve United States foreign policy objectives by... influencing public attitudes in other nations." This explicitly shifted the mission from information provision to persuasion. The USIA would also have responsibility for "advising the President, his representatives abroad, and the various departments and agencies on the implications of foreign opinion for present and contemplated United States policies, programs and official statements." In a commercial context, this is like having your marketing people in on product development. It is common now – and effective.

Edward R. Murrow died of lung cancer in 1965 at the age of 57, after receiving the Presidential Medal of Freedom, the highest award available to an American civilian, from President Johnson. (And what a great example that award is of the American instinct to "live the brand," repeating the core idea of freedom at every possible opportunity.)

Enjoy the show

For many governments, the role of culture in promoting their country presents them with a quandary. They recognize the need to show off their country's cultural attainments, but they worry that promoting culture doesn't provide the same return on investment as promoting inward investment, trade or tourism. So culture often gets treated as a not-for-profit activity, a kind of charitable obligation, rather than as a way to build competitive advantage for the nation. And in consequence, it's usually seriously underfunded.

America has never had this problem because its cultural output has been a highly marketable commodity since the late nineteenth century. It has usually paid its own way, and what's more has always been seen by American governments as one of the "hard" techniques for building the nation brand. One reason why culture is so effective at this is that consumers aren't so suspicious of it as they are of commercial messages. Even if it's popular culture, it's still art, or at least entertainment, so people relax their vigilance and don't look for hidden agendas. Until recently, Hollywood movies could get away with some fairly explicit celebrations of American values, and foreign audiences just sat back and enjoyed the show.

And cinema, music, art and literature are important because they help the nation brand to cross Murrow's "last three feet." They add colour, detail and richness to people's perception of the country, helping them get to know the place almost as well as if they'd been there. Better, in fact, because the picture that's painted is often a little idealized, and all the more magical for being intangible and incomplete.

Some of those great American brands listed in chapter 1 have done a marvellous job in sketching the outlines of Brand America: wealth, independence, ruggedness, dependability, individualism, youthfulness, fun and so on. But American films, music, literature and art have filled in the details and built Brand America into a rich and satisfying thing for hundreds of millions of people around the world to encounter, to explore and to get to know and trust over many years. No other country has ever penetrated so deeply into the lives and imaginations of so many people around the world. Almost everyone who has come into contact with books, radio, television, music, cinema, video games or branded products during the twentieth century has been touched by America, and large numbers of them have grown to love it with a passion.

From Hong Kong to Paraguay, Iceland to South Africa, every little boy who longed for a cowboy hat, a sheriff's star and a brace of pistols, and every little girl who longed for a Barbie doll, was dreaming of America. Little wonder that when they became teenagers, they reached first for American records, happily paid a bit more for American cigarettes, drank the Real Thing, and later still found it felt absolutely right working for an American firm and taking the family on holiday to Florida. Consider the intense and lifelong loyalty of *billions* of such people, and you begin to have a picture of the power and reach of Brand America.

Plausible deniability

The US government had led cultural projects abroad since at least 1938, when the Department of State's Division of Cultural Relations was established. Similarly, the Office of the Coordinator of Inter-American Affairs, set up in 1941, supported exhibitions and other artistic events in Latin America. But it was in fighting the Cold War that the federal government made a priority of showcasing American art abroad. Soviet propaganda relentlessly portrayed the US as a cultural wasteland, and with some success, so America felt it was vital to respond to this untruth in the strongest of terms.

USIA published a few magazines of its own. Their titles seem outdated now, but in their heyday periodicals including *Problems of Communism, America Illustrated and Soviet Life* were widely read and highly influential. It was public knowledge, not even an open secret, that the US government had complete editorial control over these titles. No one minded. Yet there were some in government who believed that more surreptitious means of cultural communication would be even more effective.

As it happened, the government now had just the right vehicle. As Frances Stonor Saunders writes in *Who Paid the Piper?*, her marvellous exposé of the cultural Cold War: "The founding of the CIA [in 1947] marked a dramatic overhaul of the traditional paradigms of American politics. The terms under which the Agency was established institutionalized concepts of 'the necessary lie' and 'plausible deniability' as legitimate peacetime strategies." The act that created the CIA defined its mission as coordinating military and diplomatic intelligence; nowhere was it explicitly authorized to go any further than that. The act, however, included an elastic phrase that gave the agency power to conduct "such other functions and duties" as the National Security Council (also created by the act) might direct. In the words of a later government report, successive presidents have used this clause to move the agency into "espionage, covert action, paramilitary operations, and technical intelligence collection."

The new CIA took its personality from the former OSS, which had been teasingly nicknamed "Oh so social" for its clubby elitism. Columnist Drew Pearson derided the OSS, led by Bill Donovan, as "one of the fanciest groups of dilettante diplomats, Wall Street bankers, and amateur detectives ever seen in Washington." [30] There was some truth in this. OSS operatives included, for instance, both of J. P. Morgan's sons, travel-guide publisher Eugene Fodor, Ilia Tolstoy (grandson of the novelist) and Julia Child (who ran OSS intelligence in Chungking and later became a celebrity chef). "Antoine de Saint-Exupéry," writes Saunders, "was a close friend and collaborator of Donovan's, as was Ernest Hemingway, whose son John was also in OSS." (Novelist Ian Fleming, incidentally, was also an acquaintance of Donovan's, and gave his friend early advice as the OSS was being formulated.)

State Department official George Kennan, the architect of the Marshall Plan for the reconstruction of Europe, was one of the CIA's forefathers and the author of America's doctrine of containment, which he first outlined in an anonymous article in Foreign Affairs. Kennan's political philosophy took on legal authority in late 1947 and mid-1948 when the Truman administration issued a series of top-secret National Security Council directives that he had written. What Washington's and Jefferson's speeches had been to American foreign policy prior to World War II, Kennan's NSC directives were to post-war covert engagement. "These were the documents," writes Saunders, "which piloted American intelligence into the choppy waters of secret political warfare for decades to come."

Saunders continues:

> Proceeding from the premise that the Soviet Union and its satellite countries were embarked on a programme of "vicious" covert activities to "discredit and defeat the aims and activities of the United States and other western powers," NSC-10/2 gave the highest sanction of the government to a plethora of covert operations: "propaganda, economic warfare, preventative direct action including sabotage, anti-sabotage, demolition and evacuation measures; subversion against hostile states including assistance to underground resistance movements, guerrillas and refugee liberation groups." All such activities, in the words of NSC-10/2, must be "so planned and executed that any US government responsibility for them is not evident to unauthorized persons, and that if uncovered the US government can plausibly disclaim responsibility for them."

NSC-10/2 also established a staff for covert operations, innocuously called the Office of Policy Coordination (OPC). And in 1949, Congress passed the Central Intelligence Agency Act, allowing the agency's director to spend money without having to report it publicly. Thus was born the CIA that the world has come to know, admire, fear and despise.

High culture from below

The CIA conducted its cultural operations through the OPC and especially through the so-called Congress for Cultural Freedom in Europe administered by OPC agent Michael Josselson, who had joined the CIA in 1948 as chief of covert action in its Berlin station. Josselson followed the precepts of one of his close friends and fellow operatives, composer Nicholas Nabokov (brother of *Lolita* author Vladimir): "No ideological polemic about the validity and meaning of our culture can equal the products of this culture itself." To this end, Josselson, under the banner of the Congress for Cultural Freedom – which was not publicly tied to the CIA in any way – set about promoting American culture in Europe using CIA funds.

However, as Saunders notes, "cultural freedom did not come cheap. [Through the 1950s and 1960s] the CIA was to pump tens of millions of dollars into the Congress for Cultural Freedom and related projects. With this kind of commitment, the CIA was in effect acting as America's Ministry of Culture." And minister to culture it did. "The *New York Times*," reports Saunders, "alleged in 1977 that the CIA had been involved in the publication of a least a thousand books. The Agency has never made public its publications backlist, but it is known that books in which it had an involvement" include T. S. Eliot's *The Waste Land*, Boris Pasternak's *Doctor Zhivago* and new editions of Machiavelli's *The Prince*. Writers in the employ of the CIA either wrote novels themselves or helped other aspiring writers write theirs. As a former OSS lieutenant, Eugene Fodor was happy to provide cover for CIA agents travelling around Europe, some of whose insights wound up in his travel guides. The CIA contributors, Fodor later insisted, "were all highly professional, high quality. We never let policies be smuggled into the books."

Of course, as Saunders is quick to point out, "This phenomenon of writer as spy, spy as writer, was by no means new. Somerset Maugham used his literary status as cover for assignments for the British Secret Service during the First World War.... [and] Graham Greene... once famously referred to MI5 [for which he worked during the Second World War] as 'the best travel agency in the world.'"

Novelist Richard Elman later applauded the CIA for its efforts, and for its good taste: "It is my contention," he wrote, "that the CIA not only engaged in a cultural cold war in the abstract and purely pragmatic way, but that they had very definite aims in view, and they had a very definite aesthetic: they stood for High Culture." [31]

Yankee doodles

In standing for high culture, Josselson and his colleagues were greatly helped by the emergence of the distinctly American art of abstract expressionism. According to Saunders, they viewed this form, "non-figurative and politically silent," as the antithesis of socialist realism: "precisely the kind of art the Soviets loved to hate."

As early as 1946, the *Encyclopaedia Britannica* was praising the new art as "independent, self-reliant, a true expression of the national will, spirit and character. It seems that, in aesthetic character, US art is no longer a repository of European influences, that it is not a mere amalgamate of foreign 'isms,' assembled, compiled and assimilated with lesser or greater intelligence."

At the vanguard of the new American art scene was Jackson Pollock, who embodied all the characteristics of a real American and put them into his work. As Saunders explains, "In the splurgy, random knot of lines which threaded their way across the canvas and over the edges, he seemed to be engaged in the act of rediscovering America.... [His art] was seen to uphold the great American myth of the lone voice, the intrepid individual, a tradition Hollywood enshrined in films such as [Capra's] *Mr Smith Goes to Washington*."

The CIA fostered and promoted this subversive American art in a number of ways. Saunders describes how the CIA made

The CIA promoted America's brand of art as a challenge to Soviet realist aesthetics and as a demonstration of cultural superiority.

laundered donations to the Museum of Modern Art in New York, and how the Congress for Cultural Freedom sponsored modern art exhibits all around Europe, for which MoMA supplied works by such artists as Pollock, Mark Rothko, Georgia O'Keefe, Alexander Calder and Frank Stella. (MoMA, for the record, denies having any knowledge of CIA involvement in its affairs, financially or otherwise, a claim Saunders argues persuasively is both hollow and irrelevant.)

Air superiority

In a stand-up routine in 1991, American loudmouth comedian Sam Kinison claimed to be entirely underwhelmed by Soviet Russian technological achievement. Pointing moonward, he barked mockingly: "Wanna impress me? Bring back our flag, assholes!" Kinison's gag raised a laugh as the Soviet Union lay in ruins, but it would not have seemed remotely funny on 4 October 1957, when the Soviet Union launched Sputnik, the first man-made earth-orbiting satellite, from a secret missile base in Kazakhstan. The Soviets had been talking about doing this for some time, but the actual achievement, in the words of historian Walter McDougall, "was the shot truly heard around the world... Public outcry over Sputnik had more repercussions than any event since Pearl Harbor."

Nowhere was this space-shot heard more loudly than in the United States, and it was the event that transformed a more or less cool war between East and West into full-blown Cold War. As Sputnik went up, assumptions of American technological superiority fell to earth, and national prestige became as important as military power. As Lyndon Johnson had said earlier: "One can predict with confidence that failure to master space means being second best in the crucial arena of our Cold War world. In the eyes of the world, first in space means first, period; second in space is second in everything."

The US claimed the edge again in 1962 when it released overhead imagery from a U2 reconnaissance plane that confirmed the presence of Soviet nuclear missiles in Cuba, thus resolving a perilous military and diplomatic standoff. As General David M. Shoup, commandant of the Marine Corps, put it in 1963, it was quite possibly "only by grace of God and an aerial photograph" that the world pulled through the Cuban Missile Crisis. [32]

America gained the technological edge once and for all on

Bettmann/CORBIS

The ascension of Sputnik brought American prestige back to Earth – for a few days, anyway.

20 July 1969, when Neil Armstrong stepped out of the lunar lander, took a short stroll for mankind and labelled another heavenly body with the logo of Brand America.

Less well known, but equally interesting from a brand perspective, was the soundtrack to that expensive little commercial for Brand America. Astronaut Buzz Aldrin took a tape player on the trip and became the first person to play music on the moon. "Had any other nation beaten [the US] to it," writes columnist Mark Steyn, "they'd have marked the occasion with the 'Ode to Joy' or *Also Sprach Zarathustra,* something grand and formal."

What did Aldrin choose for a soundtrack? "Fly me to the moon," the wonderful Frank Sinatra/Count Basie rendition, produced and arranged by Quincy Jones and recorded live at the

Sands Hotel in Las Vegas. "There's something very American about [that]," writes Steyn, "the sound of the American century as it broke the bounds of the planet."

There sure is.

The ideological importance of the sax solo

American jazz was played not only on the moon, but also on the Voice of America.

Willis Conover, a disc jockey from Washington, DC, was hired temporarily in 1954 to host the VOA jazz programme *Music USA,* a project some VOA officials considered frivolous. The show was an instant success, however, and became the most popular VOA offering for over 30 years. Conover's was arguably the most recognizable American voice abroad for decades, and though Smith-Mundt made him unknown in his home country, *Reader's Digest* called him "the world's favourite American."

Through more than 10,000 broadcasts, Conover played vinyl records from his own vast collection and maintained a faith in the power of his programme:

> Jazz is a classical parallel to our American political and social system. We agree in advance on the laws and customs we abide by, and having reached agreement, we are free to do whatever we wish within these constraints. It's the same with jazz. The musicians agree on the key, the harmonic changes, the tempo and the duration of the piece. Within these guidelines, they are free to play what they want. And when people in other countries hear that quality in the music, it stimulates a need for the same freedom in their lives. [33]

Conover was absolutely right. In the mid-1950s, Adam Makowicz, now a world-famous jazz pianist, was a 14-year-old music student in Poland. Every night at 11 p.m. sharp he and his friends gathered round a short-wave radio to hear the "Take the 'A' train" theme and the mellifluous voice of Conover saying "This is jazzzzzz." "Willis spoke to us distinctly and slowly," Makowicz recalls, "so that even those of us who knew very little English could understand.... That music, open to improvisation, coming from a free country, was our 'hour of freedom': music we had not known before; it was our hope and joy which helped us to survive dark days of censorship and other oppression." [34]

Two Bulgarian listeners who eventually came to the United States said of Conover: "We have been living for years with you, your voice, your music. There is absolutely no way we can describe what enormous importance you have for somebody living back there.... You are the music, you are the light, you are America."

Even today, though Conover died in 1996, there is an article in Russian called "I remember Willis" on the website *jazz.ru*. In it, a man named Leonid Pereverzev, who looks from his photo to be in his seventies, reminisces about the first time he listened to *Music USA* in the mid-1950s. "From that minute, Willis Conover, and no one else, became for me the authentic voice of the country where jazz arose... Jazz, with its unity and variety, spiritual relationships, and [message] about the right and obligation [of people] to defend their individuality." [35]

Culture at a popular price

The CIA gave its support to "serious" art and literature, but America has usually marketed itself with an overwhelming ratio of popular culture to high culture – and that's exactly right if your aim is to build a mass-market global brand rather than a nice little niche brand for a discerning elite. When American cultural exports have targeted highbrow fields, the tendency has often been a popularizing, democratizing one. In fact, almost all the great populist art forms are American in origin, or have been taken from elsewhere and popularized in the hugely fertile terrain of America's vast domestic marketplace: pop music tracing its roots back via jazz and blues through gospel and spirituals and ultimately back to Africa; musicals evolving from the operatic traditions of Italy, Russia, Germany and France; comic strips evolving from the English tradition of political satire; cinema evolving from a French invention for presenting news stories; and so on.

So America's exports have played a big part in the popularization of culture around the world. In fact, American culture has truly shaped the world we now live in through its mass democratization of taste, its tolerance of wide variations in creative and technical standards, the close relationship between culture and business, the importance of enjoyment rather than enlightenment, and the emphasis on youthful and accessible tastes in art and culture rather than the elitist, closed approach of the old world.

Commentators in Europe and elsewhere have often voiced concern at the vast quantity of popular culture that America has pumped out across the world over the past hundred years, and accuse it of dumbing down serious culture, but it has probably done just as much to keep serious culture alive. The popularizing influence of American culture has usually been an invigorating one, helping to weed out tired elements, creating new and larger audiences (and markets) for viable works, energizing the defences and reinforcing the identities of competing forms, and instilling the whole field with a sense of urgency, potential and enthusiasm.

It's no different in the commercial arena, where the arrival of attractive, accessible American brands in a foreign marketplace raises the bar for everyone. It kills off products that were unfit to survive globalization; provides a model of quality and value for the competition to match or else fail; and quite often reinforces the consumer's ultimate preference for domestic brands, some of which emerge strengthened and more efficient from the experience. It's not pleasant, and it's not without casualties, but the consumer benefits – which is the whole point of both democracy and the market economy.

Whether it's in culture or in commerce, there will always be people who mistake that very American dynamism and aggression for something evil and virulent, but on the whole it's nothing more than energy and enthusiasm – the same human genius that keeps things alive and at the forefront of social change rather than letting them be trampled by it. For example, it's easy to lament how classical singing in Western Europe has been popularized or even vandalized by American tastes (if we overlook the huge contribution made to opera by the Met and the dozens of world-class singers produced every year by American music schools, studios and opera houses). But that American hunger for popular and commercial success, that driving creativity and love of change, are much the same energy that drove Verdi and Puccini and Donizetti to produce what they produced in the first place.

Energy is always unsettling, and so are the changes it brings, but it is seldom merely destructive. America has been the powerhouse of the modern world.

© TM ® © TM ®
® © TM ® ©
© TM ® © TM ®
® © TM ® ©
© TM ® © TM ®
® © TM ® ©
© TM ® © TM ®
® © TM ® ©
© TM ® © TM ®

5

Arches Abroad: Privatizing Brand America

"America's primary weapons...are stockings, cigarettes, and other merchandise."

Josef Stalin to Zhou Enlai, 1952

"In the end we beat them with Levi 501 jeans. Seventy-two years of Communist indoctrination and propaganda was drowned out by a three-ounce Sony Walkman. A huge totalitarian system has been brought to its knees because nobody wants to wear Bulgarian shoes."

P. J. O'Rourke, 1994

America in demand

For almost thirty years, from 1961 until 1990, the 1.2 million residents of East Berlin were separated from all things western by a 96-mile concrete wall. And now they're not.

Apart from a few small sections left standing as a memorial, the Berlin Wall has left Germany and moved abroad. The UN headquarters in New York have a chunk, Buenos Aires is home to a set of massive fragments, and the garden of the Ronald Reagan Presidential Library in California fittingly displays a tall slab of it. If none of these places is convenient, just stay where you are and buy your own piece of the Berlin Wall on eBay. Think of it: pieces of the great symbol of economic oppression for sale in an Internet auction market. If ever there was a metaphor for how the American way has grown to predominance, commercially and culturally, in the past decade or two, this is as good a candidate as Disney's Little Mermaid speaking Thai, an African villager chatting on a Motorola mobile phone, or a McDonald's sign in Cyrillic.

American companies, alongside American culture, have covered the world, and they started doing it a long time ago. Singer, for example, was a pioneering global brand, setting up its first overseas branch in France in 1855. By 1890, the company had an 80 percent share of the world market in sewing machines. So grateful was the American nation that the Statue of Liberty – its most prominent brand icon – is supposed to be a likeness of Isabella Singer, wife of the company's founder. Nation brand and commercial brand, as ever, in perfect harmony.

In the early decades of the twentieth century, American brands began to travel the world more regularly. Coca-Cola's policy of issuing every GI with a bottle of Coke was certainly an original marketing strategy, and it worked. As we have seen, Hollywood and the American music industry had already prepared the

Laura Rauch/AP

Totalitarianism, flushed away. Relieve yourself on the Berlin Wall at the Main Street Station Hotel and Casino in Las Vegas.

ground culturally, and so for the remainder of the century, all American products had to do was state their country of origin. As long as the quality was adequate and the price was right, the rest was plain sailing.

Alongside Coke, iconic lifestyle brands such as Marlboro, Levi's, Zippo, Lucky Strike, Wrigley's, Wrangler and Chesterfield were America's and Hollywood's most accessible and successful carry-out. These brands were the wearable, affordable slice of America that young consumers worldwide could take away from a Hollywood or Motown experience to claim their own patch of territory in the American Dream.

Behind the Iron Curtain, even if people couldn't own the brands, they wanted the lifestyle. In the 1950s, the US Information Agency sponsored pavilion-size exhibitions in the USSR and Eastern Europe. These events drew enormous crowds eager for a peek at life beyond their closed world, and their desire for a piece of the west was furious and passionate. On the opening day of a Moscow USIA exhibit in 1959, visitors stole dozens of books from a display set up by US publishing houses. The Kremlin's demand that the replacement volumes be nailed down was rejected. [36]

After the fall of communism, the opportunities for American brands to go global multiplied. In 1997, Procter & Gamble announced that the number of consumers within its reach had increased from 1 billion to 4.5 billion in a decade, and declared that its opportunities for growth were "literally unprecedented."

As Niall Ferguson says, "Coca-Colonization...is a hackneyed catchphrase of the anti-globalization 'movement,' but it conveys a certain truth when one considers the geographical range of the soft drink company's sales today: 30 percent to North America, 24 percent to Latin America, 22 percent to Europe and the Middle East, 18 percent to Asia and 6 percent to Africa. Significantly, the Real Thing's fastest growing market is the People's

Republic of China."[37]

American brands have played a crucial part in building the world's knowledge of the country, and both industry and government have always understood the intimate relationship between America's brands and America the brand. Testifying before a Senate committee, Secretary of Defense Charles Wilson, a former head of General Motors, famously remarked: "What's good for the country is good for General Motors, and *vice versa*." It was Calvin Coolidge who pointed out, even more famously, that "the business of America is business."

But the commercial brands represent just a third of a powerful trinity of communicators that together have been the driving force behind Brand America during the past century: American brands, American culture and American media.

Hand in hand down the red carpet

As we saw in the previous chapter, America's cultural output is unusual because so much of it comes in the form of marketed products: film, television, video, books and recorded music, as well as huge amounts of associated merchandising. This means that American culture has been promoted worldwide with all the power and profitability of marketing – and with a little help from the CIA – rather than by the gentler route of cultural exchange.

Because American commerce and American culture go hand in hand, they have spread together. Disney and the other big American movie studios have a global penetration parallel to Coca-Cola's; so do many of the record labels and their artists. When they work together, as with Madonna and Pepsi, Ray-Ban and *Men in Black*, or Justin Timberlake and McDonald's, the combination is even more powerful.

Hollywood has dominated the international audio-visual

marketplace for virtually the whole of the twentieth century, writes the Australian film academic Tom O'Regan. During this period, it managed to achieve a market share of between 40 and 90 percent of national box offices in Western markets, as well as an unrivalled international presence in television markets. In the home, VCR and DVD mirror Hollywood's film market shares, and pay television creates additional demand for Hollywood-produced programming.

Over the years, many parents' groups, political movements, intellectual elites, foreign governments and foreign production industries have tried to undermine Hollywood's preeminence in their countries, says O'Regan, but without much success. Since the 1920s, many governments have set quotas on Hollywood screen presence in cinemas and on TV, taxed the profits from Hollywood screenings to support local film production, and created subsidy schemes, tax concessions and grants to encourage the production of local cinema and TV programmes. Sometimes these measures have helped the domestic production industry, but they haven't done anything to dent the popularity of the Hollywood product. Cultural protectionism is a very tricky thing to pull off except in totalitarian states.

It's not surprising there has been so much debate about America's cultural imperialism. Even if the success of its products and culture is entirely the result of people wanting and buying, it causes concern.

In China, the concern runs deep. Official commentators on cinema point out the hypocrisy and hidden agendas that they find embedded in American cultural products. The critic Chen Xiaoyun, in an article named "True Lies" after the second most successful American film in China (after *Titanic*), described "the vivid language of hegemony" as a true lie that characterized American films and the American spirit. [38] The American hero, he complains, must always represent the will of mankind, including freedom, justice and equality. Which is true enough, but if you removed all the heroes who embody universal values and represent the struggle of man against nature, or good against evil, from world literature (including Chinese literature), you wouldn't have many heroes left at the end of it.

Chen Xiaoyun concludes that Hollywood films are like opium. Once inside the imaginary world of the film, he claims, the viewer undergoes a form of hypnosis and is no longer capable of rational judgement. Another critic, Du Zhongjie, detects an "invisible hand" behind the "dreamland" presented by Hollywood, and groups Hollywood films together with such other American icons as Coca-Cola and McDonald's as links in a chain carrying American cultural imperialism across the world until eventually it takes over the minds of the target audiences. [39] In Hollywood's formulation, he claims, every region of the world has its special characteristics: Africa is presented as a barbarian land teeming with wild animals, while Asia is a land of spies and opium smokers. The only paradise is the United States itself, the land where beautiful dreams really do come true.

One of the tricks of American culture is travelling the world picking up fragments of other cultures, reworking them with an American flavour, and selling them back to the countries they came from. Disney is especially fond of this approach, selling *Winnie the Pooh* and *Alice in Wonderland* back to English children in cartoon form, and the Chinese legend of Mulan back to the Chinese. Despite getting mainly positive reviews, *Mulan* wasn't a big hit when it was released in China, although this may have been the result of unfortunate timing: the film fell victim to both the 1997 ban on American films and the outrage caused by the Americans' accidental bombing of the Chinese embassy in Belgrade in 1999. In addition, a variety of administrative regulations, including blackout dates for foreign films during key holiday periods such as Chinese New Year, continue to hinder such films. *Mulan* wasn't released in China until after children had gone back to school, and the viewers who were most enthusiastic about it had already seen it on pirated DVDs.

Hollywood often has to practise its own variety of diplomacy when promoting its products abroad. On the eve of the release of Martin Scorsese's *Kundun,* a film about the early years of the Dalai Lama, Disney hired Henry Kissinger to help explain the company's rather awkward position to the Chinese. Eventually, Disney's CEO Michael Eisner went to Beijing and met with senior Chinese officials, including propaganda chief Ding Guan'gen. Eisner pleased his hosts by agreeing to distribute two Chinese films in the US and sponsoring a Chinese acrobatic troupe in Europe, but this was little more than a gesture: one of the films – *A Time to Remember (Hongse lianren)* – is a patriotic love story set during the communist revolution and would have little interest for US audiences.

Nobody can accuse Disney or the other studios of short-termism in their strenuous efforts to open the Chinese market to American culture. Today, the entire country generates lower revenues for Hollywood than Peru does, but one day it will be America's primary trading partner.

In a letter to Disney shareholders after his return, Eisner described how impressed he had been by the obvious success of McDonald's in China, and commented that he was "completely confident that the Chinese people love Mickey no less than Big Mac." [40]

Topless beaches are culture too

When people complain about American cultural imperialism, they usually mean the branded products that have a cultural component or cultural significance: films, music, fashion and food.

It is true, says columnist Mark Steyn, that "you can fly around the world and eat at McDonald's, dress at Gap, listen to Britney Spears, and go see *Charlie's Angels 3* pretty much anywhere on the planet.... if you define 'cultural dominance' as hamburgers, America rules." But beyond the "pop" and the "fast," he maintains, America's cultural influence is actually rather limited. "On a raft of issues, from guns to religion, America is...the exception. In North American terms, it's Canadian ideas, from socialized healthcare to confiscatory taxation, that are now the norm in [both Western and emerging] democracies... In the face of this rejection of the broader American culture, the popularity of Tom Hanks isn't much consolation."

Steyn continues: "If one compares today's hyperpower with its 19th-century predecessor, Britain exported its language, law, and institutions around the world to the point where today there are dozens of countries whose political and legal cultures derive principally from London. On islands from the Caribbean to the South Pacific, you can find miniature Westminsters proudly displaying their maces and Hansards... If England is the mother of all Parliaments, America's a wealthy spinster with no urge to start dating."

Niall Ferguson thinks along similar lines: "True, 39 of the world's 81 largest telecommunications corporations are American, and around half of all the world's countries rely principally on the United States to supply their cinemas with films. But a very large proportion of Hollywood's exports go to long-standing American allies within the OECD. Apart from Japan, Asian countries – particularly India – import very few American productions. Likewise, most translations of American books and foreign users of American Internet sites are to be found in Europe and Japan. The only other region where a major channel of communication may be said to be dominated by American culture is Latin America, where 75 percent of television programs are US-made."[41]

People willingly buy into American brands and the culture and values that go with them, but actually very little of it ends up replacing local cultures. The two tend to live alongside each other, as a McDonald's in Paris or Tokyo will trade alongside a bistro or a sushi bar.

And of course the influences aren't only American. The chances are that on the other side of the McDonald's in Paris there will be a Chinese restaurant, an Irish pub or a Mexican grill. What we are witnessing may not be so much the creeping spread of American cultural imperialism, but a process of cultural cross-fertilization, which is one of the more exciting and positive effects of globalization.

Culture isn't a zero-sum game where there is only room in people's lives for a certain amount of culture and where one culture must always drive out another. The explosion of international communications means that more and more people are free to observe, learn, adopt, imitate, embrace and reject elements from a wide range of different cultures.

Yes, one of the loudest and most attractive of these is certainly American popular culture, and many people around the world have become fluent in it. But cultural exchange has always worked like this. Elements of foreign cultures fall from favour or become absorbed into their new host cultures just as foreign words get borrowed, appropriated, mispronounced and finally reinvented in other languages. In other words, people have a choice, and nothing could be more democratic, more fair or more unstoppable than this wholly pragmatic natural cultural selection.

There are a lot of American brands around, and a lot of American culture on sale. But nobody is defenceless in the face of it, and when it sticks, it's usually because people want it to stick.

VOA? No, but still three letters

The third member of Brand America's trinity of communicators, the American media, has also walked hand in hand with commerce and culture for many years, and its global impact is as visible and as profound as that of the other two. If you own the brands and you own the media channels to promote them, there is little standing between you and complete domination over any marketplace where you can distribute and transmit. If America were a corporation, it would be facing anti-trust lawsuits that would make Microsoft's difficulties pale into insignificance.

Most people who were over the age of five in 1991 will remember the TV screen as it looked during the bombing of Baghdad: the green-tinged view of the skyline, streaked with the white traces of anti-aircraft fire and pulsing with the night-vision bloom of exploding ordnance. And superimposed on this phosphorescent scene, in the corner of the screen, those three red and white initials: CNN.

In late December 1989, you could have witnessed another remarkable scene on CNN, this one taking place in Panama City. Refusing to concede power after losing a general election, Manuel Noriega had taken refuge in the Vatican embassy. The US marines sent to capture him and bring him to trial in America on charges of drug trafficking had the papal nunciature surrounded. To keep Noriega, a known fan of opera, aware of their presence (and to prevent reporters from eavesdropping on the negotiations taking place between US and Vatican officials), the marines blasted out rock 'n' roll from loudspeakers, amplified to

Bettmann/CORBIS

Hello, it's us: American paratroopers drop into Panama City.

hostile levels. They chose songs calculated to give extra offence – and a touch of humour – to the military build-up outside the embassy gates: "Hello it's me" (Todd Rundgren), "Welcome to the jungle" (Guns 'n' Roses), "Refugee" (Tom Petty), "The star-spangled banner" (Jimi Hendrix), "Crying in the chapel" (Brenda Lee) and "I fought the law and the law won" (Bobby Fuller) were on a playlist in constant rotation. [42]

When the Vatican protested that the music was harassing, and President Bush rightly decided the tactic was "irritating and petty," General Colin Powell ordered it to stop. But this remains a memorable moment in which the American military, media and culture all fell into a surreal sort of alignment.

America's dominance of international news channels is more than just a transparent medium for keeping the world informed about what the world is doing. Like Voice of America before them, CNN and the other American news channels show that sitting behind that news desk is a very influential place to be – even if you are absolutely scrupulous about presenting the facts (more or less) straight. Taking on and responsibly carrying out the job of keeping the world informed tells people a great deal about the kind of country you are.

In CNN's case, it's something a good deal more potent. Such is CNN's influence that when the protagonists in world affairs become conscious of the huge television audience watching them from the other side of that camera with the red and white logo, awaiting their every move on live television, they begin, sometimes unconsciously and sometimes deliberately, to play to that audience. Every gesture, every word, every action takes on a new significance when you know the world is watching. And if you're prepared to do something really shocking, hours of global exposure that would cost millions during paid-for advertising breaks are instantly yours, absolutely free. A minor dictator can become a global superstar in seconds. The way things are going, it won't be many years before that vast audience is invited to vote with their remote if they want the besieged dictator to be evicted from his palace.

In the last two Gulf Wars, as well as in the war on terrorism, there has been a war of news alongside the armed combat: CNN against Al-Jazeera, the voice of American truth against the voice of Arab truth. Wars have become as media focused as any other aspect of international affairs; hostility just as much as diplomacy is now irreversibly public.

And then there's MTV, which thanks to its winning recipe of branded pop culture exercises a far greater influence over young audiences than CNN does over adults. Politicians anxious to connect with future voters will go to some lengths to grab a little media space on MTV. While running for president in 1992, Bill Clinton went on MTV and answered questions about the kind of underwear he favoured ("mostly briefs" was the answer). This was mainly for a domestic audience, but the length of MTV's shadow was confirmed ten years later when Secretary of State Colin Powell joined the network for a 90-minute dialogue with young people in Brazil, India, Russia, Italy, Egypt and the United Kingdom. That broadcast reached 380 million households worldwide.

MTV, if it's an imperialist, is a subtle one. Although its format originated in the US, it does most of its programming locally, broadcasting more homegrown music than American. Like McDonald's, MTV discovered long ago that American content is foreign content if you don't come from America, and foreign content appears to have limited appeal. Most of the American TV channels now expanding across the planet have found it necessary to follow the same pattern. Discovery Network, Nickelodeon, Cartoon Network, Fox Kids and TNT have all found that television (and especially children's television) has to be a mainly domestic product if people are going to stay with it long enough to watch the ad breaks that make the money. So the American media brands find themselves in the unexpected but influential position of becoming US-branded providers of foreign culture within foreign markets.

Courtesy MTV

Beginning with its first broadcast on 1 August 1981, MTV claimed new territory for Brand America.

6

Losing the Knack:
Brand America in Decline

"There is no such thing as innocence. Innocence touched with guilt is as good a deal as you can get."

Mike Hammer in Mickey Spillane's *Kiss Me, Deadly*

"The promise of America is great, but the follow through around the world does not live up to our billing. It's no wonder the rest of the world hates us."

Mark Helmke, senior professional staff member
with the Senate Committee on Foreign Relations

Brands on the run

Not so long ago, US exporters and multinationals believed that globalization was going to make life easy for them. Theodore Levitt's confident 1983 essay in the *Harvard Business Review,* "The globalization of markets," asserted that the rise of mass transport and communications made possible by new technology was creating a world in which different cultural preferences and national tastes would disappear. Levitt predicted "a new commercial reality – the emergence of global markets for standardized consumer products on a previously unimagined scale." The essay foresaw a wonderfully smooth ride for American business around the planet, where one day you might not even need to bother translating your domestic advertising into other languages.

As Richard Tomkins, writing in the *Financial Times,* points out, Levitt had got it completely wrong. [43] Far from consolidating, consumer markets were fragmenting. People didn't want to become part of a homogenous mass, deprived of choice and force-fed standardized products. They wanted to be individuals, expressing preferences and proclaiming their identity through what Sigmund Freud once called "the narcissism of small differences."

Between 1998 and 2001, Coca-Cola experienced three years of declining net profits, had two changes of chief executive and embarked on a big restructuring. Many other American brand owners decided that the global approach was no longer valid and began to return to the old multinational model, where local managers target local audiences and develop products on a country-by-country basis.

Before it launched Diet Coke in 1982, Coca-Cola had been a one-product company for nearly a century. Now it manages a portfolio of around 400 brands in 200 countries, most of them local and free of American associations. The list includes Almdudler, Bibo, Tian Yu Di and YouKi. Even their ultimate

Isaac Menashe/ZUMA/CORBIS

This can't be good for business.

ownership is often disguised, as there's no reference to Coca-Cola on the can or bottle.

It may be that the best way for Coca-Cola to carry on making money abroad is by going local and suppressing its own brand identity, but the side-effect is that Brand America is no longer being promoted except by the flagship product. Perhaps Coca-Cola judges that its first responsibility is to its shareholders, not to the image of America.

McDonald's, too, is varying its menus and its branding to suit national tastes, and has invested in other food retailers such as Chipotle Mexican Grill in the US and Pret A Manger in the UK. But so far, it doesn't seem to have found the right recipe: in 2003 it recorded the first net loss in its 37-year history as a publicly listed company.

The writing's on the wall for US companies that continue to market their products in the brash, old-fashioned way that used to be a hallmark of some American brands. The reality of a brand's second function – as a focus for ill will as much as a reflection of good will – has begun to dawn on American brand owners. Mecca-Cola, the creation of the French entrepreneur Tawfik Mathlouthi, quickly became a *cause célèbre* in 2004 thanks to its enthusiastic reception by the global media. With the slogan "No more drinking stupid, drink with commitment," it has inspired a whole brigade of anti-American brand launches around the Muslim world. It certainly captured the Zeitgeist, even if it didn't make much of a dent in Coke's market share in Muslim countries, and a new concept was born: the protest brand.

America's old promise of wealth and liberty, the good will that so many felt towards the country for what it was trying to achieve, and the selfless way it helped its allies in times of war as well as its enemies afterwards, made people want to forgive the occasional rough edges of America, its brands, its culture and its people. America's massive importance as a trading partner helped people overlook some of its behavioural problems too. They were part of its brand character, and people even grew to love them.

But time marches on, and consumers change. The gratitude has faded as memories of the world wars have faded; the thrill and glamour of the original pop culture have worn off after decades of imitation in every country and every language; and good will has wasted away as America continues to interfere in other countries' affairs and flex its frighteningly well-developed military muscles.

Examples of the branding backlash are everywhere. In 1992 and 1998, groups of Dutch teenagers were asked whether they preferred Nike's advertising in English or Dutch. Even over this short period, opinion shifted noticeably. In 1992, a typical response was "If Nike speaks Dutch it can't be a cool brand," but in 1998, many respondents made comments such as "If you can't even figure out how to speak to me in my own language, you can't be too smart." Now Nike is a very local brand in most of its overseas markets, sponsoring local teams and catering precisely to each country's tastes in sport and style, and there's nothing overtly American about the brand except "Just do it." But even having an English-language slogan no longer necessarily means you come from an English-speaking country: it just means you're an international brand.

The World Health Organization recently reported that its efforts to complete the task of eradicating polio by 2005 were being held up in Kano province in northern Nigeria by mothers who were refusing to vaccinate their children. The culprit was a rumour that the American-made vaccine contained oestrogen in order to make their children sterile and eventually eradicate Muslims. The mothers later accepted a vaccine manufactured in Indonesia. This episode is an unwelcome twist on the theme of country of origin effect, although the technique used – a belligerent propaganda campaign waged via deliberately spread rumours – is the same one used by America's Office of Strategic Services against German troops during World War II.

We may have already passed the peak of Brand America's international appeal, and its right to brand leadership in almost every market sector. The relentless communication of American values, beliefs and lifestyle through the mass media has, of course, made foreigners highly familiar with them. After decades of intense bombardment by American culture through cinema, music, television and brands, hundreds of millions of people are now (or believe themselves to be) experts on America.

And familiarity breeds contempt, or at least indifference. America is no longer a mysterious, idealized, magical land. People travel more than they used to because it's cheaper (thanks partly to the example set by American budget airlines) and they have more leisure time (thanks partly to technology developed by American companies), and so more people than ever have been to America (thanks partly to promotions by the US Office of Travel and Tourism Industries). It's almost as cheap and easy for European parents to take their children to Disney World in Florida than to Euro Disney in Paris. America just doesn't feel so far away any more.

Familiarity also makes people question their beliefs. Views of America around the world are more complex and contradictory than before. There is still much that is positive, but also much that is negative in current perceptions of Brand America. A lot of this ambivalence is the inevitable consequence of America's position as sole global superpower: people's attitudes to absolute dominion are always mixed and uneasy.

Just stating its country of origin is no longer enough to build an American brand abroad. America isn't a premium brand in every imaginable sector any more. The world's love affair with America isn't exactly over, but it has stopped being a blind and unquestioning kind of love. Clearly, no other country offers anything like the breadth and power of Brand America, or its reputation for quality and consistency across so many different product and service areas, but several other countries now compete effectively with America in specific contexts.

A decline in the equity of America's brand doesn't mean the end of its export business, but it does signal the end of the "unfair advantage" that it once gave American companies. In future, American brands will have to compete on a more level playing field, relying more on their own brand and product qualities and less on the lazy shorthand that they come from the right place. If Brand America slips far enough in people's esteem, there is a chance that American brands will one day have to work harder than others to downplay the negative associations of their country of origin. Or else, like so many brands from poor countries today (not to mention Coca-Cola), they might need to conceal their true country of origin.

In one area, it's already happening. A US survey in August 2002 found that 68 percent of people were less likely to trust everyday brands as a result of the unscrupulous actions of Enron and WorldCom [44] – and that's everyday brands. Trust in energy traders, accountancy firms and telecommunications giants must be at rock bottom, and likely to stay there for some time. The fact that most of the corporations that have recently been disgraced are American damages Brand America. If America's economic strength and commercial primacy are part of the reason for the world's unease about the country, then any hint that this primacy has been dishonestly achieved is bound to make matters worse. The damage done is small but significant: for the first time in history, at least in a couple of business sectors, and at least for the moment, "Made in America" confers negative equity.

American industry finds itself all at once in a strange and hostile world: a world of consumers with money to spend, surrounded by good, attractive, well-branded products at sensible prices, more and more of which aren't American. It's a world where "Made in America" is suddenly not the only offering, nor automatically the most exciting, nor the best; it's just one choice among many.

By contrast, communism posed but a pale threat to America's brand leadership; those Bulgarian shoes of which P. J. O'Rourke speaks were really no contest. The challenger today is capitalism: not America's military foes, but the disaffection of its consumers and the skill and determination of its competitors.

Affairs of substance

These foreign waters are even choppier for the ship of state, and American public diplomacy is struggling against what is now regularly described as a rising tide of anti-American feeling.

Naomi Klein, best known for *No Logo*, her diatribe against globalization, has criticized the Bush administration's talk of rebranding America on the grounds that "America's problem is not with its brand – which could scarcely be stronger – but with its product." According to Klein, what makes people angry with America is its false promises, the fact that it says one thing and does another. And she's right: matching product to promise is the first responsibility of any good marketer.

People unfamiliar with marketing may be surprised to hear marketers talking about getting the product right. But one old and very good definition of marketing is "matching the strengths of the organization to the needs of the marketplace" – in other words, making sure you have a market, and that you're connecting with it. If your product isn't what the market wants or needs, then you don't have a business, as marketers, who spend much of their time talking to consumers and finding out what they want and need, should know full well.

Good companies understand this, make sure they have marketers who understand it too, and put them in positions where they can directly influence the development of the product, its quality, how and where it's distributed, and how it's sold. Some exceptional companies that understand that their real long-term success depends not just on selling lots of products but on building a powerful brand make sure that they have brand-aware marketers on the board, where they can help define corporate strategy according to the changing needs of consumers. In fact, many truly successful companies are run by people with a marketing background, or at least a strong instinctive understanding of marketing principles.

The best way for a company to get no value from marketing is to see it as a coat of glossy paint that you simply slap over whatever the product people come up with. Companies that view marketing in this way are places where you hear expressions like "dumb consumers." For them, business is all about making a product and then tricking people into buying it.

Even though many countries claim to appreciate the importance of their brands these days, and may have elaborate programmes for managing them, there's often a limited understanding of marketing behind it all. For these places, "nation brand" is just modern jargon for public relations and advertising – propaganda, in other words. Everything comes down to communications: putting a shiny coat of PR over whatever the government decides in its wisdom is the right thing to do at any moment.

There are many problems with this approach, but the biggest is that it makes truthfulness as a policy impossible. If the job of marketing is simply to make everything sound good, then the country's messages could at any point be truth or lies or a mixture of the two, depending on the decisions of the government on any particular day. Some days, it'll be a simple matter of telling the world about something good; others, it'll be what George Orwell called "the defence of the indefensible." As we said before, you can only lie about your product once: as soon as people find you out (and they *will* find you out), they will never trust your word again. Lying damages a brand beyond repair.

This is why managing a country's brand is a far more ambitious and radical project than it may at first appear. It starts with the premise that today's community of nations is open, transparent and substantially democratic – in many ways, like a marketplace – and that the state's reputation is therefore of critical importance. It means adopting a policy of evaluating every action of the state in terms of both its practical consequences and its effect on the state's good name, because that good name is its most valuable possession. Is it the *right thing* for that state to do? Is it in character?

Some governments do this instinctively when dealing with their own citizens, believing that it's just as important to consider whether the people will like, understand and respect their decisions as it is to consider whether they are the right decisions. But today, all governments need to do this for the *world's* citizens. Public affairs has become an international affair.

As we've seen, America was founded by people with an excellent natural grasp of these principles, and over the centuries there have often been marketers, born or trained, with a seat on the board of Brand America. There are certainly some in the State Department today: Howard Cincotta of the Office of International Information Programs gives an excellent definition of public diplomacy in HTH Worldwide's Summer 2003 *Quarterly Advisor:*

> First, it's not public relations. The job of public diplomacy is not to put a high gloss or spin on American policies, but to inform diverse foreign audiences about the administration's policies and priorities, to win their understanding, and to build the coalitions necessary for meaningful international action. In other words, it's policy, not PR. To be effective, public diplomacy and policy must be inseparable.

But Washington's behaviour in recent years more and more resembles one of those cynical old-fashioned companies that thinks the only job of marketing is to spruce up policy before it's presented to the public.

Modern American governments seem to overvalue and undervalue marketing at the same time. They undervalue it because they don't see it as having anything useful to contribute to the way the country is run: it's hard to imagine a twenty-first-century State Department asking for or even listening to advice about how the invasion of Iraq or the imposition of steel tariffs could affect the country's brand equity. But at the same time they overvalue marketing because of their naïve faith in its magical ability to turn lead into gold – to perform the impossible and trick the world into thinking that bad behaviour is good.

What *have* we got here?

The problem with matching words to deeds is that governments (and not just US governments) have such a strong tendency to believe that everything they do is right.

On 16 December 1998, without telling the congressional intelligence committees (or running it past the UN), President Clinton ordered a four-day missile and bomb attack on targets in Iraq. "If we turn our backs on [Saddam's] defiance," said the president, referring to the expulsion of UN weapons inspectors six weeks earlier, "the credibility of US power as a check against Saddam will be destroyed."

Some say that the timing of the attacks was suspicious, as Congress was due to vote the next day on whether to impeach the president for lying under oath to the grand jury investigating his alleged sexual misconduct with a subordinate. Clinton may not always have appreciated how closely his behaviour was connected to his own and to America's reputation, but he clearly did understand the effect that America's military actions had on its reputation.

Several months earlier, in February 1998, Secretary of State

CORBIS SYGMA

President Clinton, flanked by symbolism, announces Operation Desert Fox on 16 December 1998.

Madeleine Albright defended potential future strikes against Iraq by saying: "If we have to use force, it is because we are America. We are the indispensable nation. We stand tall. We see further into the future."

You might take Albright's words as evidence of American arrogance, but according to Chalmers Johnson, author of *Blowback*, there was nothing new or surprising about the ideals that informed them: "We Americans deeply believe that our role in the world is virtuous – that our actions are almost invariably for the good of others as well as ourselves. Even when our country's actions have led to disaster we assume that the motives behind them were honorable." [45]

For a number of reasons, including the indecisiveness of the United Nations and the military weakness of continental Europe, American-led interventions have become more frequent in recent years. This might be a factor behind the US's reluctance, much to the world's chagrin, to ratify the treaty on the International Court of Justice; being out on the line so much, it fears a disproportionate subjection to international law.

The American habit of well-intentioned meddling, particularly in the praiseworthy but tricky pursuit of establishing "acceptable" democratic regimes, has a long history. In 1913, when General Victoriano Huerta seized power in Mexico after the assassination of the liberal premier Francisco Madero, the US refused to recognize the new government. In London, British Foreign Secretary Sir Edward Grey had the following exchange with American Ambassador Walter Page:

> *Grey:* Suppose you have to intervene, what then?
>
> *Page:* Make 'em vote and live by their decisions.
>
> *Grey:* But suppose they will not so live?
>
> *Page:* We'll go in and make 'em vote again.
>
> *Grey:* And keep this up for 200 years?
>
> *Page:* Yes. The United States will be here for 200 years and it can continue to shoot men for that little space till they learn to vote and to rule themselves. [46]

Even before 9/11, there were more than 250,000 American military personnel stationed in 130 countries outside the US. In some of these places they are welcomed; in others, less so. In Okinawa, Japan, where the US has maintained an enormous base since the end of World War II, the military dominates the local real estate and the local economy. Even if most of the time community relations are satisfactory in these areas, now and then something bad happens. American soldiers raped a 12-year-old schoolgirl in Okinawa in September 1995, and in February 1998 US marines accidentally flew a plane through the cable of a cable car in Italy, sending twenty skiers to their deaths. Because of incidents like these, which can occur from time to time, it's unreasonable to expect local attitudes toward America's presence ever to be better than mixed.

If it's not sending military people, America is sending military stuff. The US is the largest arms dealer in the world. Whatever upside there may be to this, it will inevitably stir up hostility when a missile stamped "Made in USA" destroys a Palestinian's home, especially if it was launched by an Israeli-piloted helicopter that also came from America. But here too is a brand lesson: you'll never please everybody. One of the demands of the terrorists who kidnapped *Wall Street Journal* reporter Daniel Pearl, before they slit his throat on camera and distributed the video, was that the US resume the sale of F-16s to Pakistan.

When it isn't shipping troops or weapons, the US is wiring – or withholding – money. It does so either directly through foreign aid, or indirectly through such organizations as the International Monetary Fund, described by Chalmers Johnson as "essentially a covert arm of the US Treasury, yet beyond congressional oversight because it is formally an international organization." Similar accusations are often levelled at the World Bank, whose head is directly appointed by the US president. And like some omnipotent credit-rating agency, US or IMF decisions reverberate through the financial markets, with a secondary impact on affected nations that can exceed the magnitude of the initial one.

On the subject of ratings, America also wields vast economic influence through its three biggest credit-rating agencies, Moody's, Standard & Poor's and Fitch. These firms dominate the world market in sovereign ratings, a way of grading a country's solvency that is used by investors the world over to decide which countries are safe to invest in and which aren't. It is no exaggeration to say that the fate of nations hangs on the way these firms decide to brand them. To make matters worse, as the academic Michael Kunczik pointed out in a 2003 lecture to the Croatian Diplomatic Academy, their conclusions are arrived at by methods that are not even published: they are considered trade secrets.

By the time the Iraq situation arose in 2002 and 2003, it was, for many people, just the latest and greatest in a long line of reasons to feel angry with America.

Of course, a brand is the sum total of many factors, a stockpile of accumulated debits and credits. As with the Rosenberg case, which in 1953 became the rallying point for anyone and everyone with a bone to pick with America, fifty years from now the outrage over Iraq will probably be seen as a manifestation of a whole load of gripes – some legitimate, some not – all rolled into one and labelled "No blood for oil."

Having a powerful brand magnifies faults as well as virtues. If you're describing a country that flouts international law at its own convenience, violates treaties when it pleases, and doesn't always get UN approval for its military actions, you could just as well be talking about, say, France as America. The difference is that France isn't the gorilla in the world's living room. Unlike America, it isn't the world's biggest brand.

The cliché that actions speak louder than words holds true in nation branding as much as anywhere else. It can be argued that where US foreign policy is concerned, what has happened is that the image of America has finally caught up with the non-ideal reality.

For Americans who trust their nation's intentions implicitly, this can be a bewildering realization. US diplomat David Newsom, in his 1988 book *Diplomacy and the American Democracy*, explains: "[American practitioners of public diplomacy] imagined the international public environment to be fundamentally sympathetic to the American message. Instead [the] message has, like official policies, encountered a complex and occasionally hostile reception... [Americans are prone to thinking] that if their policies are not acceptable to others, it is because the nation has not been sufficiently effective in 'selling' the policies." [47]

In other words, the problem is not so much the persuasiveness of the message as the credibility of the messenger. The majority of America's brand communications these days fall on deaf or tuned-out ears.

Sharing the right values?

Former advertising executive Charlotte Beers, appointed Under-secretary of State for Public Diplomacy soon after the terrorist attacks of 11 September 2001, made history by launching the first TV advertising campaign for Brand America, which was broadcast to predominantly Muslim countries in the following year. Her appointment, heralded by Secretary of State Colin Powell's unforgettable comments at her confirmation hearing ("Well, guess what? She got me to buy Uncle Ben's rice, and so there's nothing wrong with getting somebody who knows how to sell something") was controversial from the outset. But as we've seen, there's nothing new about such roles within the federal government. Nor is it even new for the advertising industry to be involved at this level. In the 1950s, the Advertising Council, the trade organization for the American ad industry, was according to Hans Tuch a "valued advisor" to USIA management, and it still is today.

Beers' campaign was dubbed the Shared Values Initiative. Its first phase consisted of five mini-documentaries for television, radio and print about Muslim life in America, designed to run during Ramadan. The spots featured a Muslim-American baker, doctor, school teacher, journalist and firefighter talking positively about their experience of living and working in the United States. Each spot ends with the line, "A message from the Council of American Muslims for Understanding and the American People." The idea was to show that Muslims lead happy and rewarding lives in America, and can follow their religion freely.

Aired on television in Pakistan, Malaysia, Indonesia and Kuwait, in Kenya and Tanzania through the US embassies, and on Pan-Arab television covering Saudi Arabia, Kuwait, UAE, Bahrain, Oman, Qatar, Jordan, Lebanon and Egypt, the spots reached an estimated audience of 288 million people. The campaign was also extended by speaking tours, town-hall meetings, print publications, radio broadcasts and Arab outreach programmes. But the ads researched inconclusively and were widely criticized. The project was terminated amidst vague and contradictory statements. In March 2003, Beers resigned her position on health grounds.

Beers had been anxious to stress to critics that the purpose of the campaign was not to talk about US foreign policy, but to focus on a single message of religious tolerance. It was designed, she said, in order to "redefine who America is...not only for ourselves...but also for the outside world."

Tolerance is a funny word. The idea of tolerating somebody sounds so grudging and is often an expression of political correctness, that grimmest of liberal doctrines. But it looks as if the main problem was that the Shared Values Initiative was yet another product of the "to know us is to love us" school of public diplomacy. Simply showing that Muslims are happily integrated into American society isn't even a good first step towards tackling the real worries of Muslims abroad about America's policies. It seems to be saying "And before you start criticizing us, we just want to say that we totally understand Muslims; we've got lots of them back home."

Howard Cincotta counters this objection, arguing:

> Some commentators responded to this shared values initiative by saying, in effect: "Everyone knows about America's freedoms and religious tolerance – it's irrelevant to the pressing issues of the day." Yet every international poll of attitudes in the Middle East and Asia consistently suggests the contrary. Western-educated elites, including exchange students, may be familiar with American values and culture, these polls conclude, but the broader populations clearly are not. Instead, many regard America as irreligious and hostile to Islam, espousing a culture antithetical to their culture and values. In such an environment, it is unlikely that our policy messages will even be heard, much less judged fairly.

It may well be true that the campaign's audience isn't aware of America's tolerance of religious minorities, and it certainly would be a good thing to convince Muslims that America has no hostility towards their religion. But America's insistence that it is "tolerant" of Islam does nothing to counter the more serious charge that American culture is antithetical to Islamic culture. Arguably, nothing can.

Simply pointing out that immigrants to America are allowed to practise their own faith in the privacy of their own neighbourhoods misses a fundamental point about Islam. Unlike modern Christianity, Islam isn't just a religious doctrine, a "Saturday religion": it's a complete spiritual, philosophical, moral, political, legal, economic and social system. For this reason, America's traditional separation of religion and state is anathema to Islam. Pointing out how American Muslims are allowed to pray at their local mosque may just be emphasizing to Muslims abroad that this is an infidel country where the fundamental religious rules of life are considered trivial – little more than a private indulgence or a weekly entertainment, and secondary to the "state creed" of capitalism.

And the conclusion that might be drawn from America's strange decision to go on television to talk about happy Muslims in America – rather than tackle the issues of US foreign policy in the Middle East, which is really the only question on people's minds at this point – is that America is implying that this vision of a watered-down, secularized, capitalist Islam is the model that Muslims the world over should espouse. In fact, it might look exactly as if that's what America is trying to sell.

To a follower of Osama bin Laden or any other so-called fundamentalist Muslim, the immigrant Muslims who choose to settle in a country like America, far from representing a model to be listened to or admired, are seen as traitors to Islam who have sold out to capitalism, and the fact that they are tolerated in American society reflects well neither on them nor on America.

The decision to use TV advertising spots as a medium for the message may have made things even worse. The television commercial is by no means as familiar or neutral a form of communication to people in the Middle East and Africa as it is to Americans. It's the means by which products are sold to you, itself an imported American idea – in fact, if you want to be hard line about it, the classic instrument of American cultural and economic imperialism. To use such a vehicle to present friendly socio-cultural messages about religious acceptance seems likely to cripple the initiative right from the start.

This reading is by no means the only possible interpretation of the Shared Values Initiative, and it's not intended as an explanation of why the campaign appears not to have gone down too well in many Muslim countries. What it does show is that without a *complete* understanding of the cultural, political, social and spiritual context in which the audience operates, even apparently very simple, innocent and friendly messages can take on a meaning very far removed from the actual intention.

In good public diplomacy, and good marketing, giving people information about yourself has its place, but understanding your audience has a far higher priority than trying to force them to understand you. The basis of effective communication is seeing yourself *absolutely* objectively, and *absolutely* in the way that your audiences see you – one of the hardest things for any person, company or country to do, especially one that has been utterly convinced of the unique virtue of its own world view for nearly three hundred years.

Exhaustive knowledge of the audience, its tastes, culture, language, world view, morals, politics and society, is only the beginning. Above all, you need to understand what Sicco van Gelder calls the "mental lenses and filters" of brand perception through which your audience views you, and take a long, hard look at yourself through them. [48]

Know your audience is advice that wouldn't go amiss in higher circles, either. After the breaking of the story about abuse of Iraqi prisoners by US soldiers at Abu Ghraib prison, President Bush apologized not in an Iraqi forum, but in an interview with the official Egyptian daily *Al-Ahram*. According to columnist Deroy Murdock, "This gaffe was akin to having President Bush communicate US policy to Venezuelans by granting an exclusive sit-down with *El Mercurio* of Santiago, Chile. The *Al-Ahram* misstep suggests that the United States government cannot distinguish among 'the little brown people' of the Middle East." [49]

In reality, public diplomacy directed at your enemies or your enemies' friends in times of conflict is extremely unlikely to achieve anything positive. If people are in the habit of seeing America as their enemy, it's naïve to hope that they will interpret any of its messages or actions favourably. The more conciliatory or humble these messages appear to be, the more convinced the audience will be that they harbour some cunningly concealed threat or propaganda.

America just isn't used to being hated, and doesn't know how to deal with it. Some of its audiences see it as a sinister and brutal regime, and that's the image of itself that America understandably has most trouble comprehending. But comprehend it must.

A good starting point would be simply to appreciate how large, powerful and frightening America appears to smaller, poorer, less "sophisticated" countries – especially if they see its armies on television night and day, pounding the life out of a nearby country. Under such circumstances, that humble, friendly, propitiatory tone of voice can only appear sinister, insincere or grotesque.

There's only one thing scarier than a bully, and that's a bully that wants to be loved.

The hard edge of soft power

America may have lost some of its skill at managing its own brand, but when it comes to branding other countries, it's still a world leader. Ever since President Reagan fired off the epithet "evil empire" at the Soviet Union in 1983, it's been clear that America possesses a weapon of mass persuasion against which there is virtually no defence. Because America carries so much media clout, and because the utterances of US presidents are in any case instantly reported in every corner of the world, a single well-chosen phrase can attach to a country, get massive publicity, and become extremely difficult to shake off.

The term "rogue state" is another recent favourite of American presidents, but it has never really stuck to any country in particular; in fact, critics often use it against the United States itself. "Failed state," when used by a US president, carries enough weight virtually to put a country out of business. An attempt to use the more politically correct phrase "state of concern" under the Clinton administration proved short lived, presumably because there was no warhead attached.

More recently, and even more infamously, the phrase "axis of evil" was coined by President Bush in his State of the Union speech in January 2002. This "three for the price of one" brand enjoyed more worldwide media exposure than any commercial slogan; within days, it was bigger than "Coke adds life" or "Just do it." It was also something a little worse than political rhetoric, or the ideological exaggeration of Reagan's comment. By borrowing the term "axis" from the Axis powers of World War II, Bush implied an alliance between Iran, Iraq and North Korea that suited his political aims but had little basis in fact.

And if these phrases are the belligerent-branding equivalent of ballistic missiles, there are also the occasional hand grenades, more often than not lobbed at friends and allies, such as "Old Europe," and the extraordinary "cheese-eating surrender monkeys" (not an official federal weapon, this one – it was coined by an American journalist and given worldwide airplay anyway).

One wonders what Arthur Miller would have to say about these tags. Looking back at the way the US changed post-war allegiances and alliances with such insouciance, the author of *Death of a Salesman* wrote in 1987: "It seemed to me in later years that this wrenching shift, this ripping off of Good and Evil labels from one nation and pasting them onto another had done something to wither the very notion of a world even theoretically moral. If last month's friend could so quickly become this month's enemy, what depth of reality could good and evil have?"

We hate you, but please send us *Baywatch*

A country's brand is a complex thing, and it doesn't suddenly fail just because one or two points of the hexagon lose their influence. In fact, one of the reasons why a good brand is such an asset, for countries as well as companies, is that it makes you more resilient. A good reputation means people are slower to believe bad things about you, and it gives you a period of grace to resolve a crisis before they lose faith in your product or your country.

And people are perfectly able to compartmentalize their feelings about countries. Most people are intelligent enough to understand that foreign policy is something created by governments, not by people. It's common for people to despise a country's policies but love its products. Many describe America as utterly decadent, yet consume its culture voraciously.

In fact, if you're ever overseas and meet someone who claims to hate everything about America, just ask them what's their favourite movie or where they would most like to go abroad and study.

But if the balance continues to shift against America, people might start to see even its best-loved products in a new light. Even American entertainment, looked at from a certain viewpoint, can do more harm than good to Brand America.

In 2002, Boston University professors Margaret and Melvin DeFleur carried out a study called "The next generation's image of Americans" in which they surveyed 1,259 high school students (median age: 17) in Saudi Arabia, Bahrain, South Korea, Mexico, China, Spain, Taiwan, the Dominican Republic, Pakistan, Nigeria, Italy and Argentina. "Evaluating statements about characteristics, values and behaviour of Americans as people (not the US government, its actions or policies), the teenagers generally said that Americans are violent, materialistic, want to dominate, are disrespectful of people unlike them, not generous, unconcerned about the poor, lack strong family values

REUTERS/Claro Cortes IV CC

For better or worse, the American government has often let US corporations manage US foreign relations.

and are not peaceful. They also believe many Americans engage in criminal activities." In an interview, Melvin DeFleur revealed that male respondents were often heard to say they would like to have a romantic relationship with an American woman so they could go to bed on the first date. Few of those surveyed had ever had direct contact with an American, and only 12 percent had visited the United States. Their views about America were shaped almost entirely by American TV, movies, music and video games. Says Melvin DeFleur: "These results suggest that pop culture, rather than foreign policy, is the true culprit of anti-Americanism."

Given the source of the problem, DeFleur thinks public diplomacy from on high is of little value as a remedy. "I don't think that the government can play much of a role [out of respect for First Amendment guarantees of free speech]... I think the answer is voluntary change on the part of [the entertainment producers]." Is this far-fetched? Maybe, but as DeFleur points out, "There is a pattern here. You remember the Ford Explorer, and the problem they had with it rolling over. That is one case where they were creating a product that harmed people. At first they denied it, but then public pressure was put on them...eventually they came into compliance." [50] Here as anywhere else, brands are answerable to consumers.

Business for Diplomatic Action, a non-governmental pressure group representing American companies and the marketing community, is less hopeful. The group's mission statement contains this analysis of America's current reputation:

> The alarming rise in anti-American sentiment represents a looming crisis for US businesses, especially for US brands marketed abroad. Even though much resentment of our country currently centers on our foreign policy, much does not.

> Other root causes include the perception that we are arrogant and insensitive as a people, that our culture has become all-pervasive, and that the global business expansion on the part of US companies has been exploitive.
>
> Research confirms the global erosion of trust and preference for a wide range of American brands. One in four consumers in the Asia-Pacific region says they avoid using US brands. "Power Brand" scores for most US brands measured by Roper were down in 2003 for the first time. The latest research from NOP World shows significant drops in "trust" and "honesty" for four leading US brands over the past year. A number of restaurants in Germany will no longer serve Coke, sell Marlboros or accept American Express cards. Thirty-six thousand people responded to a "Boycott Brand America" Web site in Vancouver, British Columbia. While many US corporations have not yet experienced a direct hit on their bottom lines, attitude always precedes behavior, which means a negative impact on sales is only a matter of time.

It looks very much as if Brand America is in need of a new strategy.

Too little too soon

Many of America's commercial, cultural and media brands are doing exactly what a well-managed brand should do when a changing consumer culture threatens its position: they are reviewing their brand strategy. The fact that more of them appear to be dropping overt references to their country of origin is not a good sign for Brand America. But all good marketers know that the customer is king, and if the customer doesn't rate "Made in America," then you don't put it on the product.

The other points of the Brand America hexagon, and in particular the policy makers, don't seem to have got the message yet. Successive US governments have fallen into the habit of performing international relations in a way that more and more resembles the secretive, highly politicized, elite diplomacy of the old European powers that Franklin so despised.

And a bit like parents who use the television as a babysitter, the US government in the past decade or so has ceded much of the management of its national reputation to the private sector. It has defaulted on its responsibilities as brand steward, causing the other points of the hexagon – culture and trade in particular – to have a disproportionate sway over perceptions of America abroad. Although the results are mixed, many now feel it was a mistake to dismantle America's public diplomacy structures along with the Berlin Wall.

"Ever since the Cold War ended," laments *Finding America's Voice,* a 2003 report by the Council on Foreign Relations, "Washington has been stripping bare the institutions designed to share US culture and values. Overseas projects such as English-language libraries have been dismantled, and the number of scholarships for foreign students to study at US institutions has dropped from 20,000 a year in the 1980s to 900 today."

Joseph Nye says, "With the end of the Cold War, soft power

Richard T. Nowitz/CORBIS

No imitations.

Franklin has proved a tough act to follow for his modern-day counterparts.

seemed expendable, and Americans became more interested in saving money than in investing in soft power. Between 1989 and 1999, the budget of the United States Information Agency (USIA) decreased 10 percent; resources for its mission in Indonesia, the world's largest Muslim nation, were cut in half. By the time it was taken over by the State Department at the end of the decade, USIA had only 6,715 employees (compared to 12,000 at its peak in the mid-1960s). During the Cold War, radio broadcasts funded by Washington reached half the Soviet population and 70 to 80 percent of the population in Eastern Europe every week; on the eve of the September 11 attacks, a mere 2 percent of Arabs listened to the Voice of America."[51]

America has more power than it has ever wielded before, but less and less of a brand advantage. It has more ability and opportunity to practise coercion, and less and less willingness on the part of others to be persuaded.

7

Just Do It: Rejuvenating Brand America

"There was no corner of the globe in which America was not a familiar word, but as to our aims, our ideals, our social and industrial progress, our struggles and our achievements, there were the most absolute and disheartening misunderstandings and misconceptions."

George Creel, 1922

"In projecting America's messages, Washington must be especially mindful of something that every good salesman understands – if you do not trust the messenger, you do not trust the message."

Report by a task force of the Council on Foreign Relations, 2003

Human nature's a funny thing. When we see somebody struggling to achieve greatness, we empathize with them, we cheer them on, we admire them. But let them attain greatness and keep hold of it for a while, and we usually turn against them.

America, like all market leaders, is now facing the consequences of having fulfilled most of its ambitions. Its dominant market position is described as a monopoly; every action it takes to protect its commercial interests provokes shrieks of protest; its (usually well-intentioned and occasionally bungled) attempts to live up to its responsibilities as sole superpower and maintain a bit of order around the planet are called empire building; its confidence is called arrogance; and its good acts are seen as hypocritical. When it really does do something wrong, all hell breaks loose.

America's mistakes are typical of market leaders too. Complacency sets in, and there's a tendency to forget or undervalue the qualities and behaviours that built the brand in the first place. Genuine arrogance combines with a reluctance to get to grips with understanding the marketplace in depth and detail, creating an inability to deal sensitively with friends, foes and customers. A certain amount of disorganization and incoherence becomes apparent in the management of the business. (Again, this is often the price of success in big organizations; consistent and well-coordinated group behaviour is needed to get to the top, but once you are there, it easily slips.) And you see a lack of clear thinking – or at least clear *communication* of the thinking – about where things go from here.

It's hard to behave like a challenger when nobody is challenging you, and it's difficult to keep getting better when you think you're already the best.

America needs to rediscover its brand instinct, and live by the principles that most American companies never forgot: clarity and firmness of purpose and message; sensitivity to the needs of different audiences around the world; a simple and attractive positioning; transparent and ethical behaviour in the organization as well as in the products (a new requirement, but it's fundamental and can't be ignored); coordination between the stakeholders. And to tie it all together and really start to take control of its image, America needs to adopt a disciplined, comprehensive approach to national brand strategy.

Strategize and share

First, America needs to be entirely clear about where the country is now, and how it is perceived, in depth, by the rest of the world.

Next, it needs to have a clear, viable and sustainable vision for where the country is going, its reason for continuing to exist (yes, every country needs one), and its future role and position in the community of nations.

The brand strategy is simply the map that shows America how it is going to travel from the former to the latter. Having a proper strategy is like that chemistry experiment where you sprinkle iron filings onto a sheet of paper. It's just a mound of black stuff until you put a magnet underneath the paper, and then in an instant, magically, the filings form themselves into a perfect infinity symbol.

The strategy is the aligning principle that makes order out of chaos. It provides all the stakeholders – not just the government – with a simple set of guidelines about what is the right thing to do at every moment. Selecting between options is suddenly a great deal simpler and more objective: does this take us in the right direction? If so, it gains a priority point. If not, it doesn't.

The vision and the strategy need to be broadly shared by the country at large, otherwise it's virtually impossible that any change will occur.

Know the long from the short of it

It's essential to recognize the difference between the long-term management or rebuilding of Brand America – measured in decades, not months or years – and the fixing of negative perceptions in the short- to medium-term. If it's the latter, we need to find out whether these perceptions are justified or not. If they are, can we help people to see them in context and in proportion so they don't write off the whole country?

Is the short-term fixing so urgent that it's really just crisis management? If so, it's more a matter of public relations than brand strategy. And how much of the task is specifically about countering hostile propaganda, as State Department officials sometimes indicate?

Chances are, it will be a mixture of all these. Each one needs to be approached in its own way; some need to be tackled by different groups of people; and a proper framework is needed so that every type of activity fits clearly into the overall strategy.

In the longer term, if it continues to work well, the brand strategy becomes self-fulfilling. Once a critical mass of aligned behaviour occurs, it starts to inspire people spontaneously to take new and more creative actions that are instinctively "on brand." And then conformity to the brand strategy becomes automatic. The country brand becomes powerful and positive enough for brand owners to *want* to display it on their products once again, now that it adds to rather than detracts from their own brand equity.

Once they start to kick in, the effects of a powerful national brand strategy are self-multiplying. If the strategy is properly and fully shared it can be a source of renewed purpose and even of common identity for the whole country.

Coordinate stakeholder communications

America's nation-branding hexagon is no longer properly joined up. That's partly because no single body has the remit and the authority to achieve this.

What's needed is a single Brand America working group with members drawn from government, civil society, NGOs, entertainment, the media, small and large businesses, the foreign service, tourism, culture and the arts, religion, academia and education. The working group must have real influence, real budgets and a direct reporting line to the president.

There's been a lot of controversy about the meagreness of public diplomacy budgets in the United States. Commentators have observed that the budget for the Shared Values Initiative, at $15 milllion, was a tiny sum compared to what even a medium-sized corporation would spend on a regional advertising campaign. But in fact money is a red herring.

As we have shown, America spends trillions every year creating an image of itself without even realizing it, through the huge variety of actions and communications of its various stakeholders. Even a limited amount of agreement and coordination between these parties would effectively leverage a proportion of that gigantic investment and steer it towards rebuilding Brand America. That effective spend on America's brand image could run to tens of billions of dollars. Any effort and expense that goes towards aligning the communications of these stakeholders will probably achieve far more than any attempt to create dedicated messages for Brand America.

American brands need to be involved in the cause of building Brand America because they are among the country's most powerful ambassadors. The difficulty is finding ways to engage their owners to make a contribution to the cause when so many of them now prefer to appear global or even foreign rather than American.

It's a question of *persuasion* again: no American government could force Hollywood or General Motors or Jennifer Lopez to incorporate the branding of America into their own activities more than they already do (and one hopes that no American government would want to try). Part of the solution is to offer them a national message that is so compelling in its own right that they will see it as a worthwhile addition to their own. If the project is ambitious but achievable, creative but practical, and appealing without being superficial, there's a good chance they will *want* to help. It's not hard to show that a strong Brand America is in their own commercial best interests, and one of the wonderful things about America, unlike many other countries, is that you can also rely on people's patriotism to help things along.

It makes sense to start with the brand ambassadors who *need* Brand America to be powerful and positive: the ones whose brands are inextricably linked to their country of origin; the ones that don't have the choice of simply dropping their American associations when they no longer work in their favour. And when it comes to coordinating the points of the nation-branding hexagon, remember that some join up more naturally than others. For example, it's much easier for United States tourism to collaborate and align its messages with American culture than with the software industry or universities. But the universities and software companies can easily align their messages with the promotion of inward investment.

Right now, the stakeholders of Brand USA are just a scattering of stars in the night sky; America needs to help people see them once again as a friendly constellation. If it doesn't, the world will join them up in its own way, and who knows whether they'll see a scorpion, a mad bull or a giant brandishing a sword.

Live the brand

As we have seen, "living the brand" is shorthand for a concept that is, in principle, very simple. The general population as well as the private and public sectors need to agree with, subscribe to and *enact* the country's vision of what it is, what it stands for and where it's going. At least, they need to do this as far as it's possible in a vigorous democracy.

It hardly needs stressing that this isn't a marketing trick; it's one of the biggest and most important jobs of a good government. With the right leadership, it can and does happen. And having a shared and widely acknowledged problem is a big help: it may be that the wave of negative sentiment America is now facing will serve as a unifying force for Americans to do something about it.

Those sections of Smith-Mundt relating to domestic dissemination of propaganda need to be repealed. They don't do any good any more, and in the internet age there's nothing to stop Americans finding out what the State Department is saying to the world. In that sense, repealing them won't make any difference. Where it will help is by allowing the government once again to discuss with the domestic audience what's being done in their name.

Showcase on-brand behaviour

No matter how much or how little America spends on trying to conduct public diplomacy through paid-for media, it's likely to be money wasted. Underfunded campaigns simply won't achieve enough impact: if an audience has only one or two opportunities to view a commercial or a print ad, it's highly unlikely to make a lasting impression on them. And unless the audience is very well-defined and very small, multiple opportunities to view cost

REUTERS/Saeed Khan/Pool

When America does good, it now gets less attention because it clashes with prevailing perceptions.

staggering amounts of money. On the other hand, an overfunded campaign – the kind that could make the sort of splash a Nike or a Coca-Cola achieves – is likely to be counterproductive, because if America's basic problem is that people think it's a bully, then using overwhelming force will confirm that impression and reinforce people's resistance to the message.

Microsoft, a company that has the misfortune of sharing some brand characteristics with its country of origin, barely advertises at all. This is partly because, like America, Microsoft doesn't need to: awareness and sales are not the issue, and it knows that flooding the media with expensive marketing communications would call attention to the company's wealth, power and self-satisfaction (the three brand qualities it least needs to stress). Advertising is essential for organizations that need to make themselves look bigger; it is has limited uses for those that don't.

The primary role of paid-for communications in public diplomacy is to *support public diplomacy actions,* not to try to create changes in attitude. As we have said, good stories don't get out on their own; so that they don't go to waste, they need to be properly showcased and presented in a context where they can do most good to the brand. Good, culturally sensitive and media-friendly communications are essential here.

Communications are also essential for shorter-term activities such as news management and countering negative propaganda. It's important that this kind of tactical activity, no matter how urgent, is always in harmony with the overall brand strategy. That way, no effort is wasted and as few messages as possible go out that contradict or fail to support the main thrust of the brand.

Balance the bad with the good

As Senator Chuck Hagel, a member of the Senate Foreign Relations Committee, said recently (with a note of exasperation in his voice), "There's no question that this country has done more for more people in more ways than any nation on the face of the Earth, any nation in history." [52] Perhaps it would be productive for America to be *angrier* about the fact that the good it does is contributing so little to its brand. But this isn't the fault of the audience for failing to draw the right conclusions; it's America's fault for not helping them to do so.

In many cases, the problem isn't that people don't know about the good things America does. Most people have heard about the vast amounts of money, labour, innovation and expertise that America and Americans contribute to aid and development, poverty reduction, healthcare and education in the third world, the building of schools and mosques in Iraq, and so on. But if managing America's reputation abroad is about placing weights on both sides of the scales so that the good things counterbalance the bad, then America is somehow not placing the facts squarely on the scales, because they're not tipping the balance. People can't square the positive side of America's behaviour with its military interventions, so they don't know what to do with the knowledge, and simply discard it. Merely piling on more information about America's good works is pointless when it clashes with the audience's beliefs.

Good public diplomacy doesn't try to do this. It finds out when, where and why that balance between the good and the bad is going awry, and helps audiences to create the right balance in their own minds. It shows them how to link the stories together into a picture of the country that's more complete, more fair, more helpful and probably more interesting too.

It's usually a waste of energy contradicting your audience, however tempting it might be when they're repeating terrible lies about you. People hang on to their prejudices because they are convenient and in harmony with the spirit of the times, and they certainly aren't going to abandon their views just because you tell them to. It's like martial arts: if you have a heavy opponent running towards you, the worst thing you can do is try to stop him in his tracks; you'll just get flattened. Use his forward momentum to get him to go where you want him to go: trip him up. Don't try to take people too far in one step. Start with their prejudices: show you understand them and where they come from, add a little extra interesting information, and build a bridge to a nearby subject that's more neutral. Leave it at that. Next time, start with the neutral subject...and so on.

It takes patience because you are fighting against one of the toughest facts in society: good stories simply don't have the same power as bad ones. Audiences – and the media, whose job it is to give audiences the content they want – are always most interested in stories that fit their prejudices about countries. Most stories that don't reaffirm prejudices are an irritant; even if they get printed, they'll probably be discarded by the reader.

It's important to understand what makes a story work. Bad news stories, like Abu Ghraib or Guantánamo Bay, carry their own power. As readers, we assume that if a story reflects badly on a country, then it *must* be true because it's not in that country's interest for us to know about it. We think we've found a rip in the curtain of official truth, and of course that's irresistible, and we do whatever we can to wrench out more of this precious truth. Good stories, on the other hand, sound like advertisements, so we take them, like advertisements, with a large pinch of salt.

Many brand leaders end up in this situation. If you say something bad about them it must be true, and if you say something good it must be a lie.

There's only one way out: to make the truth irresistible. If the good stories about America are inherently powerful, striking and unusual enough, well told and full of human interest, without any heavy-handed moralizing or neat conclusions tacked on, then each good story becomes its own brand, and effectively self-promotes. But they must all match up with each other and with an underlying truthful, credible theme; they must clearly *add up to something.*

Don't forget that the best way for a democracy to prove it's democratic is *not* by filling the airwaves with protestations about its values. One of the most effective ways for America to prove – rather than just claim – that it is the home of free speech and tolerance is not just to tolerate but actively to encourage dissenting voices in its mainstream media. It's always the bravest and toughest thing to do, but the mere existence of a movie like Michael Moore's *Fahrenheit 9/11* probably does more to convince the sceptical that America really is a democratic country than any amount of carefully crafted positive propaganda.

Let the people build the brand

The millions of immigrants to America over the centuries, and their gratitude to the country, are the true foundation of modern America's success as a global brand. That sense of gratitude at having been welcomed in your hour of need, yet allowed to be yourself once you're there, with the country demanding nothing in return but your allegiance to the flag and your honest enterprise, is the greatest driver of benign nationalism one can imagine. The effects of that gratitude resonate down the generations.

Ordinary people who feel this kind of attachment to their country make the most sincere, energetic and effective ambassadors that a government could wish for. You don't have to pay them; they do it for love. They are incredibly effective because nobody doubts their sincerity. And there are tens of millions of them doing it every day. In fact, the responsibility for the promotion of America could happily rest on their shoulders.

If only they got out more. At present, only 20 percent of Americans have passports. This is a cultural pattern that probably won't change overnight, but the educational establishment needs to think about ensuring that future generations of Americans not only travel more, but travel with cultural sensitivity and open eyes and ears, engaging in happy and mutually productive exchanges with other people. They will come back appreciating their country better too, having learned something of the way that others see it. As O. Henry wrote: "You can't appreciate home till you've left it, money till it's spent, your wife until she's joined a woman's club, nor Old Glory till you see it hanging on a broomstick on a shanty of a consul in a foreign town."

Finding ways of engaging the millions of Americans who live abroad, and making them into public diplomats, is another important task. Several countries, including Ireland and Scotland, have achieved great benefits by concentrating on their diasporas and making use of the fact that people's loyalty towards a distant motherland is often stronger than when they're at home: absence makes the heart grow fonder.

Tourism has an important role to play too, because it's harder to harbour ill feelings towards a country you've visited, especially if you enjoyed your stay and people were friendly to you when you got there. Clearly the US Office of Travel and Tourism Industries already does everything it can to stem the decline in foreign visitors, but countries that have understood the link between selling vacations and converting foreign visitors into willing ambassadors for their country brand have often found that this different perspective yields new ideas and new links with other stakeholders.

There are innovative suggestions for how citizens can help with short-term public diplomacy needs as well. A Council on Foreign Relations task force recommends establishing a Public Diplomacy Reserve Corps: "This agency, patterned on the Federal Emergency Management Agency's disaster-relief model, would augment US and overseas operations, mandate an action plan, a skills database, periodic training, updated security clearances, simplified reentry regulations, and modification of temporary appointment requirements; and recruit prestigious private sector experts from relevant professions for short-term assignments."

Clearly, good ideas aren't lacking, and plenty of people in America understand what's needed to get Brand America back on track. But the thing that will tie all these loose ends together, ramp the smaller initiatives up into bigger ones, coalesce the willing and actually create change on a big scale is the brand idea itself. This is the banner under which all these people and organizations need to unite. At the moment, everybody is being expected to give their time and their support to something that sounds rather boring called US public diplomacy. This is a little like asking consumers around the world to refresh themselves with a sweet, fizzy brown fluid.

The task of branding America must itself be branded, or it will never gain sufficient momentum to achieve the enormous task it faces.

Integrate marketing and policy making

If public diplomacy is to work properly, it will be necessary to make the formulation of foreign policy more sensitive to brand issues. In the words of the CFR task force, "This doesn't mean that America should change its policies to suit others' wishes. This is unrealistic. But it does mean that Washington must be aware of the cost of anti-Americanism and form and communicate US foreign policy with the brand consequences fully in mind."

As long as 50 years ago, Murrow urged that "public diplomacy officials be included when foreign policies are made for several reasons: to ensure that policymakers are aware of the likely reaction of foreign publics to a forthcoming policy; to advise how best to convincingly communicate polices to foreign audiences; and to ensure that US diplomats are prepared to articulate policies before they are announced."

The end result, according to the CFR task force statement, is that "public diplomacy [becomes] an integral part of foreign policy, not something that comes afterwards to sell the foreign policy or to respond to criticism after the fact. It should not decide foreign policy issues, but it must be taken into consideration at the same time as foreign policy is being made. In this way it would help define optimum foreign policies as well as explain how US policies fit the values and interests of other nations, and not just those of Americans."

Remember how the British seemed to arrive at a concept of America long before the colonists did, simply because they were at a distance and able to see what was going on more objectively. In this sense, America's foreign audiences may understand some things about Brand America better than Americans do. That's another reason why it's important to listen to them carefully: in many ways, they know what it's right for America to do.

Just as the state belongs to the people, not the government, the brand belongs to the consumers, not the company.

Reconsider the role of culture and education

As Mark Leonard of the UK's Foreign Policy Centre puts it, effective public diplomacy is mainly about "engaging people with one's country...strengthening ties." [53] The Fulbright scholarships mentioned in chapter 4 are a good example of this kind of activity. Educating people one at a time may seem like tending to drops in the ocean when there's a whole world to be persuaded of your country's values, but the ocean is made up of drops, and anyway – to take a leaf out of Franklin's book – if you target the opinion formers, you are influencing many more people than the individual in front of you. Such schemes plant a seed of understanding, affection and gratitude that may stay within people for the rest of their life. Their loyalty towards the country and their desire and ability to convey it to other people become virtually unshakeable.

In many ways, Fulbright is the perfect model for public diplomacy: it's the only approach that demonstrably works, almost without fail. So the big task for America today is to work out how personal, lasting and profound changes in people's views can be carried out on a vastly larger scale than the 25,000 or so Fulbright and international visitor exchanges that take place each year. Clearly, America is never going to be able to create real engagement with more than a tiny fraction of the world's population. But the aim must be to do so as deeply as possible with as many people as possible, because as we said earlier, people who like brands act as marketers for them.

The USIA's "Amerika Hauser," mentioned in chapter 4, serve as a good example of how this personal engagement can be extended to larger audiences. Unlike the United States, Britain has persisted with its work of cultural and educational engagement abroad through the British Council, which still brings huge benefits to the country. The British Council operates in 220 towns and cities in 110 countries, receives 8.5 million visitors to its libraries every year and employs 1,700 teachers in 126 centres overseas. Britain's international image is suffering some similar setbacks to America's, but the British Council's influence is clearly identifiable in some of the areas where Britain's reputation is more positive than America's.

With America's vastly greater resources, a modern version of the USIA could achieve an extraordinary amount.

Brand America at the crossroads

Finally, there's the question of all that power.

Absolute power corrupts absolutely, goes the maxim, and considering how much power America wields it's pretty remarkable that it has wielded it with such restraint over the past century or so. But that fine resolution of "peace, commerce, and honest friendship with all nations, entangling alliances with none" all too soon gave way to reluctant interventions in other people's disputes. This in turn gradually gave way to some well-intentioned meddling; and over the past fifty years or so, circumstances have conspired to create a widespread impression that the meddling isn't so well-intentioned any more.

Today, the consensus is growing that America throws its weight around culturally, politically, economically and militarily. That paragon of soft power, the only empire in the history of world to be built on peaceful trade rather than theft and oppression, has begun to slip the velvet glove from the iron fist.

The trouble is that once you start using coercion, persuasion stops working. Soft power can be used only when there is trust. Trade is a two-way process, and selling depends on consumers *allowing* themselves to be persuaded. They won't do that if they fear you have the alternative of coercion, and are prepared to use it. Instead of welcoming you in, they'll be more likely to defend themselves from you. So the community of nations is doing exactly what it should: keeping a very close check on a country that wields phenomenal power. In other words, it's a standoff.

But America isn't like the other powerful nations that have stood at the crossroads in the past. When the Roman, British, Ottoman, Mongol, Soviet and Greek empires reached crisis points in their histories, it's a safe bet that not many people apart from their own citizens cared much about what became of them. America is different. Just how different is beautifully evoked in this extract from a recent book by British author Jenny Diski:

> As a child in fifties London, America was as distant a reality to me as ancient Egypt, yet present in my life in a way that those who had carved the remnants of mighty statuary I knew from my visits to the British Museum could never be. Distant is not quite the word. America was like the moon: its remoteness was irrelevant, what mattered was the light it bathed me in, its universal but private reach. The moon was the moon, and mine; familiar and personal shining over me wherever I was, whenever I looked at it.

> America, too, was light. It beamed above my head from the cinema projection booth, particles dancing in its rays, ungraspable as a ghost, but resolving finally on the screen into gigantic images of a world I longed for, yet only half believed in. If I walked directly in front of the screen and got caught in its light, my very own shadow was projected up there with the bold and the beautiful, the lovers, the adventurers, the underworld, the mean streets, the promising and punishing streets, the all-singing, all-dancing, all-laughing and crying world of what we then called the flicks. People in the audience shouted at me to duck down and get out of the way as if I hadn't realized what had happened, but I knew exactly what I was doing. I wanted to be in the way of all that. [54]

America has a *market* out there – hundreds of millions of people who have grown up with feelings as strong as this. It may sound trivial or sentimental, but America really did build an empire by making people love it, by giving them wonderful dreams and unbelievable products and the greatest show on earth. In consequence, Brand America has a vast global consumer base out there that, deep down inside, *cares what happens to it.*

In other words, the world wants Brand America back.

America, the first nation to make democracy and free trade the cornerstones of its national identity and purpose, has always understood that branding is an inherently peaceful and humanistic approach to international relations. It's based on competition, choice and consumer power, and these concepts are intimately linked to the freedom and power of the individual in a democracy. For this reason it's far more likely to result in lasting world peace than a statecraft based on territory, economic power, ideology, politics or religion.

Best of all, the brand approach offers America the ultimate prize if it does things well: the chance to be top dog *and* be loved.

A superpower can't achieve this; a brand leader can.

John Springer Collection/CORBIS

High noon for Brand America

ENDNOTES

1 "Country Names as Brands: Symbolic meaning and capital flows" available at: *http://www.sba.muohio.edu/abas/1999/pantzajo.pdf.*

2 "Benjamin Franklin in France" in Hubert H. Bancroft, editor, *The Great Republic by the Master Historians* available at: *http://www.publicbookshelf.com/public_html/The_Great_Republic_By_the_Master_Historians_Vol_II/benjaminf_hc.html.*

3 William H. Helfand, "Advertising Health to the People," available at: *http://www.librarycompany.org/doctor/helfand.html.*

4 James Harvey Young, *The Toadstool Millionaires: A social history of patent medicines in America before federal regulation,*Princeton Press, New Jersey, 1961.

5 Richard L. Merritt, *Symbols of American Community 1735-1775,* Yale University Press, New Haven, 1966, p. 144.

6 Quoted in Samuel P. Huntington, *The Clash of Civilizations and the Remaking of World Order,* Simon & Schuster, London, 1998, p. 111.

7 Walter Isaacson, *Benjamin Franklin: An American life,* Simon & Schuster, New York, 2003, p. 339.

8 Isaacson, p. 325.

9 Monteagle Stearns, *Talking to Strangers: Improving American diplomacy at home and abroad,* Princeton University Press, Princeton, 1999, p. 5.

10 Joseph Nye ,*The Paradox of American Power,* Oxford University Press, Oxford, 2002.

11 Stearns, p. 20.

12 Nancy Snow, *Information War: American propaganda, free speech and opinion control since 9/11,* Seven Stories Press, New York, 2003, p. 25.

13 *http://www.propagandacritic.com/articles/ww1.cpi.html.*

14 George Creel, *How We Advertised America,* Harper and Brothers, New York, 1920; excerpts available at: *www.historytools.org/sources/creel.html.*

15 George Creel, "The Battle in the Air Lanes," *Popular Radio,* September 1922, pp. 3-10, available at: *http://earlyradio.us/1922air.htm*

16 *http://www.prfirms.org/resources/news/rally120501.asp.*

17 Snow, p. 56.

18 Hans N. Tuch, *Communicating with the World: US public diplomacy overseas,* St Martin's Press, New York, 1990, p. 3.

19 John Brown, "The purposes and cross-purposes of American public diplomacy," University of North Carolina, 15 August 2002, available at: *http://www.unc.edu/depts/diplomat/archives_roll/2002_07-09/brown_pubdipl/brown_pubdipl.html.*

20 Clayton D. Laurie, *The Propaganda Warriors: America's crusade against Nazi Germany,* University of Kansas Press, Lawrence, 1996, p. 136.

21 US Army Professional Writing Collection, available at: *http://www.army.mil/professionalwriting/volumes/volume1/september_2003/9_03_1.html.*

22 Alan L. Heil, Jr, *Voice of America: A history*, Columbia University Press, New York, 2003, p. 36.
23 Quoted in John Brown.
24 Snow, p. 125.
25 Tuch, p. 16.
26 Quoted in Tuch, p. 23.
27 Edwin J Feulner *et al.*, "Regaining America's Voice Overseas: A conference on US public diplomacy," Heritage Lecture #817, Heritage Foundation, Washington, DC, 13 January 2004, p. 15.
28 Frances Stonor Saunders, *Who Paid the Piper?: The CIA and the cultural Cold War*, Granta Books, London, 1999, p. 191.
29 George Grow, "People in America: Edward R. Murrow," VOA broadcast, 4 July 2004, available at *www.voanews.com*.
30 Saunders, p. 34.
31 Saunders, p. 234.
32 Stephen N. Whiting, "Policy, Influence, and Diplomacy: Space as a national power element," thesis presented to the faculty of the School of Advanced Airpower Studies, Air University, Maxwell Air Force Base Alabama, June 2002, p. 27.
33 Heil, p. 288.
34 Heil, p. 290.
35 Available at: *http://www.jazz.ru/mag/123/conover.htm*.
36 Wilson Dizard, "Remember USIA," *Foreign Service Journal*, July-August 2003, p. 60.
37 Niall Ferguson, *Colossus: The rise and fall of the American empire*, Penguin, London, 2004, p. 19.
38 Chen Xiaoyun, "Zhenshi huangyan: Meiguo dianying de huoyu baquan," [True Lies: The vivid language of hegemony of American films], *Zhongguo dianying bao* [China Film News], 12 August 1999, p. 2.
39 Du Zhongjie, "Menghuan bei hou you zhi kanbujian de shou," [There is an invisible hand behind the dreamland], *Zhongguo dianying bao* [China Film News], 12 August 1999, p. 2.
40 *http://www.asiaweek.com/asiaweek/99/0205/feat4.html*.
41 Ferguson, p. 21.
42 United States Southern Command, Public Affairs After Action Report Supplement, "Operation Just Cause," 20 December 1989 – 31 January 1990, available at: *http://www.gwu.edu/~nsarchiv/nsa/DOCUMENT/950206.htm*.
43 Richard Tomkins, "Anti-war sentiment is likely to give fresh impetus to the waning supremacy of US brands," *Financial Times*, 27 March 2003.
44 The research was sponsored by Madison-based branding firm Lindsay, Stone and Briggs, and AcuPOLL Precision Research. Source: *Marketing* magazine.
45 Chalmers Johnson, *Blowback: The costs and consequences of American empire*, Time Warner, London, 2002, p. 224.
46 D. C. M. Platt, *Finance, Trade, and Politics in British Foreign Policy 1815-1914*, Oxford, 1969, pp. 326ff, as cited by Ferguson.

47 Quoted in Tuch, p. 113.
48 Sicco van Gelder, *Global Brand Strategy,* Kogan Page, London, 2004.
49 Deroy Murdock, "Where are the communications majors?," *National Review Online,* 14 May 2004.
50 R. Nolan, "Global Q&A: The next generation's image of Americans: A conversation with Melvin DeFleur," Foreign Policy Association, 2004, available at: *http://www.fpa.org/topics_info2414/topics_info_show.htm?doc_id=139388.*
51 Joseph S. Nye, Jr, "The decline of America's soft power: Why Washington should worry," *Foreign Affairs,* May/June 2004, pp. 16-20.
52 Feulner, p. 4.
53 Mark Leonard *et al., Public Diplomacy,* Foreign Policy Centre, London, 2002.
54 Jenny Diski, *Stranger on a Train: Daydreaming and smoking around America with interruptions,* Virago, London, 2002, p. 8.

BIBLIOGRAPHY

Simon Anholt, *Another One Bites the Grass: Making sense of international advertising*, Wiley, New York, 2000.

Simon Anholt, *Brand New Justice: The upside of global branding*, Butterworth-Heinemann, Oxford, 2003.

Hubert H. Bancroft, editor, "Benjamin Franklin in France," *The Great Republic by the Master Historians*, available at: *http://www.publicbookshelf.com/public_html/The_Great_Republic_By_the_Master_Historians_Vol_II/benjaminf_hc.html.*

John Brown, "The purposes and cross-purposes of American public diplomacy," University of North Carolina, 15 August 2002, available at: *http://www.unc.edu/depts/diplomat/archives_roll/2002_07-09/brown_pubdipl/brown_pubdipl.html.*

J. Hector St John de Crevecoeur, *Letters from an American Farmer*, edited by W. P. Trent and Ludwig Lewisohn, Duffield, New York, 1904.

Jenny Diski, *Stranger on a Train: Daydreaming and smoking around America with interruptions*, Virago, London, 2002.

Wilson Dizard, Jr, "Remember USIA," *Foreign Service Journal*, July-August 2003.

Xiaoyun Chen, "Zhenshi huangyan: Meiguo dianying de huoyu baquan" [True Lies: The vivid language of hegemony of American films], *Zhongguo dianying bao* [China Film News], 12 August 1999.

George Creel, "The battle in the air lanes," *Popular Radio,* September 1922, available at: *http://earlyradio.us/1922air.htm.*

George Creel, *How We Advertised America,* Harper and Brothers, New York, 1920, excerpts available at *www.historytools.org/sources/creel.html.*

Zhongjie Du, "Menghuan bei hou you zhi kanbujian de shou" [There is an invisible hand behind the dreamland], *Zhongguo dianying bao* [China Film News], 12 August 1999, p. 2.

Niall Ferguson, *Colossus: The rise and fall of the American empire,* Penguin, London, 2004.

Edwin J. Feulner *et al.,* "Regaining America's voice overseas: A conference on US public diplomacy," Heritage Lecture #817, Heritage Foundation, Washington, DC, 13 January 2004.

Jami A. Fullerton and Alice Kendrick, *The Shared Values Initiative: The US government's use of advertising to fight the war on terrorism,* unpublished draft, 2004.

Thomas Gad and Anette Rosencreutz, *Managing Brand Me: How to build your personal brand,* Momentum, Alton, Hampshire, 2002.

George Grow, "People in America: Edward R. Murrow," VOA broadcast, 4 July 2004, available at *www.voanews.com.*

John Hanc, "Rallying the public: A look back at government efforts to 'spin' a war," *Newsday,* New York, 5 December 2001, p. B3.

Alan L. Heil, Jr, *Voice of America: A history* Columbia University Press, New York, 2003.

Samuel P. Huntington, *The Clash of Civilizations and the Remaking of World Order,* Simon & Schuster, London, 1998.

Samuel P. Huntington, *Who Are We?: America's great debate,* Simon & Schuster, London, 2004.

Walter Isaacson, *Benjamin Franklin: An American life,* Simon & Schuster, New York, 2003.

Chalmers Johnson, *Blowback: The costs and consequences of American empire,* Time Warner, London, 2002.

Stephen C. Johnson, "Improving US public diplomacy toward the Middle East," Heritage Lecture #838, Heritage Foundation, Washington, DC, 24 May 2004.

Clayton D. Laurie, *The Propaganda Warriors: America's crusade against Nazi Germany,* University of Kansas Press, Lawrence, 1996.

Mark Leonard, *et al., Public Diplomacy,* The Foreign Policy Centre, London, 2002.

Theodore Levitt, "The globalization of markets," *Harvard Business Review,* May-June 1983.

Deroy Murdock, "Where are the communications majors?" *National Review Online,* 14 May 2004.

R. Nolan, "Global Q&A: The next generation's image of Americans: A conversation with

Melvin DeFleur," Foreign Policy Association, 2004, available at: *http://www.fpa.org/topics_info2414/topics_info_show.htm?doc_id=139388.*

Joseph Nye, *The Paradox of American Power,* Oxford University Press, Oxford, 2002.

Joseph S. Nye, Jr, "The decline of America's soft power: Why Washington should worry," *Foreign Affairs,* May/June 2004, pp. 16-20.

P. J. O'Rourke, *Peace Kills: America's fun new imperialism,* Atlantic Monthly Press, New York, 2004.

Wally Olins, *Corporate Identity: Making business strategy visible through design,* Thames & Hudson, London, 1989.

Peter G. Peterson *et al., Finding America's Voice: A strategy for reinvigorating US public diplomacy,* Council on Foreign Relations, New York, 2003.

Stefan Pollklas, "Democrats in America: de Tocqueville and Lieber," American Studies Group, University of Virginia, 18 February 1998, available at:
http://xroads.virginia.edu/~hyper/detoc/democrats/print.html.

Henry Porter, "How to save Brand America," *Observer,* 23 March 2003.

Frances Stonor Saunders, *Who Paid the Piper?: The CIA and the cultural Cold War,* Granta, London, 1999.

Nancy Snow, *Information War: American propaganda, free speech and opinion control since 9/11,* Seven Stories Press, New York, 2003.

Monteagle Stearns, *Talking to Strangers: Improving American diplomacy at home and abroad,* Princeton University Press, Princeton, 1999.

Mark Steyn, "Hamburgers yes, federalism no," *Jerusalem Post,* 30 June 2004.

Richard Tomkins, "Anti-war sentiment is likely to give fresh impetus to the waning supremacy of US brands," *Financial Times,* 27 March 2003.

Hans N. Tuch, *Communicating with the World: US public diplomacy overseas,* St Martin's Press, New York, 1990.

United States Southern Command, Public Affairs After Action Report Supplement, "Operation Just Cause," 20 December 1989-31 January 1990, available at:
http://www.gwu.edu/~nsarchiv/nsa/DOCUMENT/950206.htm.

David Usborne, "Brand America: Iraq's corporate collateral damage," *The Agribusiness Examiner,* 21 July 2003.

Stephen N. Whiting, "Policy, influence, and diplomacy: Space as a national power element," thesis presented to the faculty of the School of Advanced Airpower Studies, Air University, Maxwell Air Force Base Alabama, June 2002.

www.jazz.ru

www.nancysnow.com

www.steynonline.com

www.whitechapelbellfoundry.co.uk/liberty.htm

Titles in the Series

Arsenal, Winning Together: The Story of the Arsenal brand by John Simmons and Matt Simmons

America, The Mother of All Brands by Simon Anholt and Jeremy Hildreth

Beckham, The Story of How brand Beckham was built by Andy Milligan

Dyson, The Domestic Engineer: How Dyson changed the meaning of cleaning by Iain Carruthers

Google, The surprising success of the Search Engine by Neil Taylor

Guiness, The colourful Story of a Black and white brand by Mark Griffiths

Harry Potter, Brand magic of the boy Wizard by Stephen Brown

Ikea, A Brand for all the People by Elen Lewis

Innocent, Building a brand from nothing but fruits by John Simmons

Starbucks, How they made Starbucks a Home away from Home by John Simmons

Scotch Whisky, Creative Fire: The Story of Scotland's Greatest Export by Stuart Delves